The Scottish Ospreys

PHILIP BROWN

The Scottish Ospreys

From Extinction to Survival

With a Foreword by
GEORGE WATERSTON, O.B.E.

HEINEMANN : LONDON

William Heinemann Ltd
10 Upper Grosvenor Street, London W1X 9PA

LONDON MELBOURNE TORONTO
JOHANNESBURG AUCKLAND

First published in Great Britain 1979

SBN 434 08910 9

Printed and bound in Great Britain by
Morrison & Gibb Ltd, London and Edinburgh

This book is dedicated, in affection and high regard, to Miss Isabel MacDonald of Inchdrein, a remarkable lady who foster-mothered scores of lucky children, yet still found time to welcome so many of us who watched over the ospreys, with apparently inexhaustible kindness and a quiet encouragement that gave many of us renewed faith, strength and enthusiasm when the fates were conspiring against us.

Books by
PHILIP BROWN

Reed-Warblers *(with M. G. Davies)*
The Return of the Osprey *(with George Waterston)*
Birds of Prey
Birds in the Balance
Uncle Whiskers
The Cat that Came in from the Cold

Contents

Illustrations

* from *A Fauna of the North-West Highlands and Skye* by J. A. Harvie-Brown, 1904.
† from *Tour in Sutherlandshire* by Charles St John, 1849.

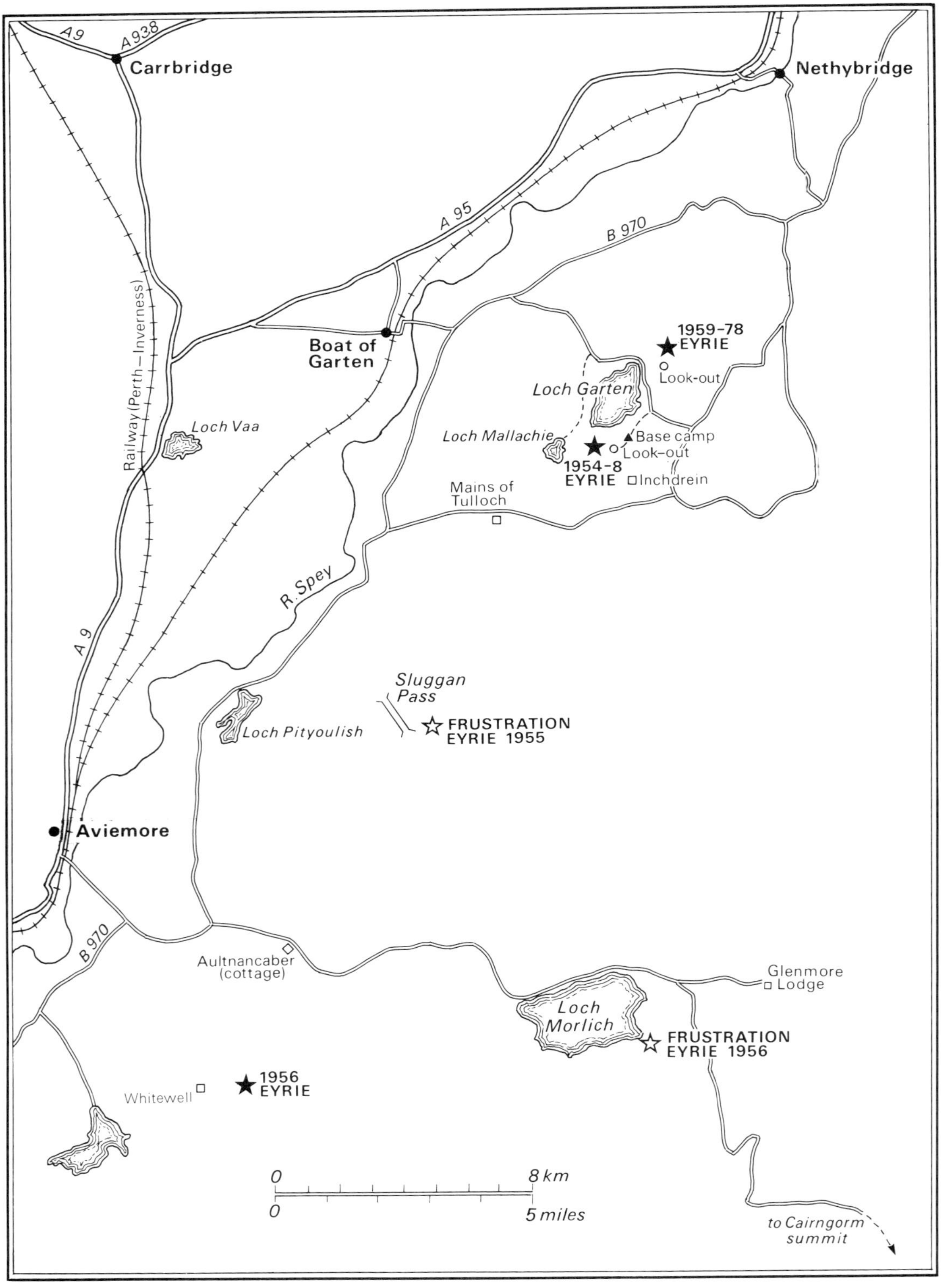
A9
A938
Carrbridge
Nethybridge
A 95
B 970
Railway (Perth – Inverness)
Boat of Garten
1959-78 EYRIE
Look-out
Loch Garten
Loch Vaa
Loch Mallachie
Base camp
Look-out
1954-8 EYRIE
Inchdrein
Mains of Tulloch
R. Spey
A 9
Sluggan Pass
FRUSTRATION EYRIE 1955
Loch Pityoulish
Aviemore
B 970
Aultnancaber (cottage)
Glenmore Lodge
Loch Morlich
FRUSTRATION EYRIE 1956
1956 EYRIE
Whitewell
0
8 km
0
5 miles
to Cairngorm summit

SPEYSIDE

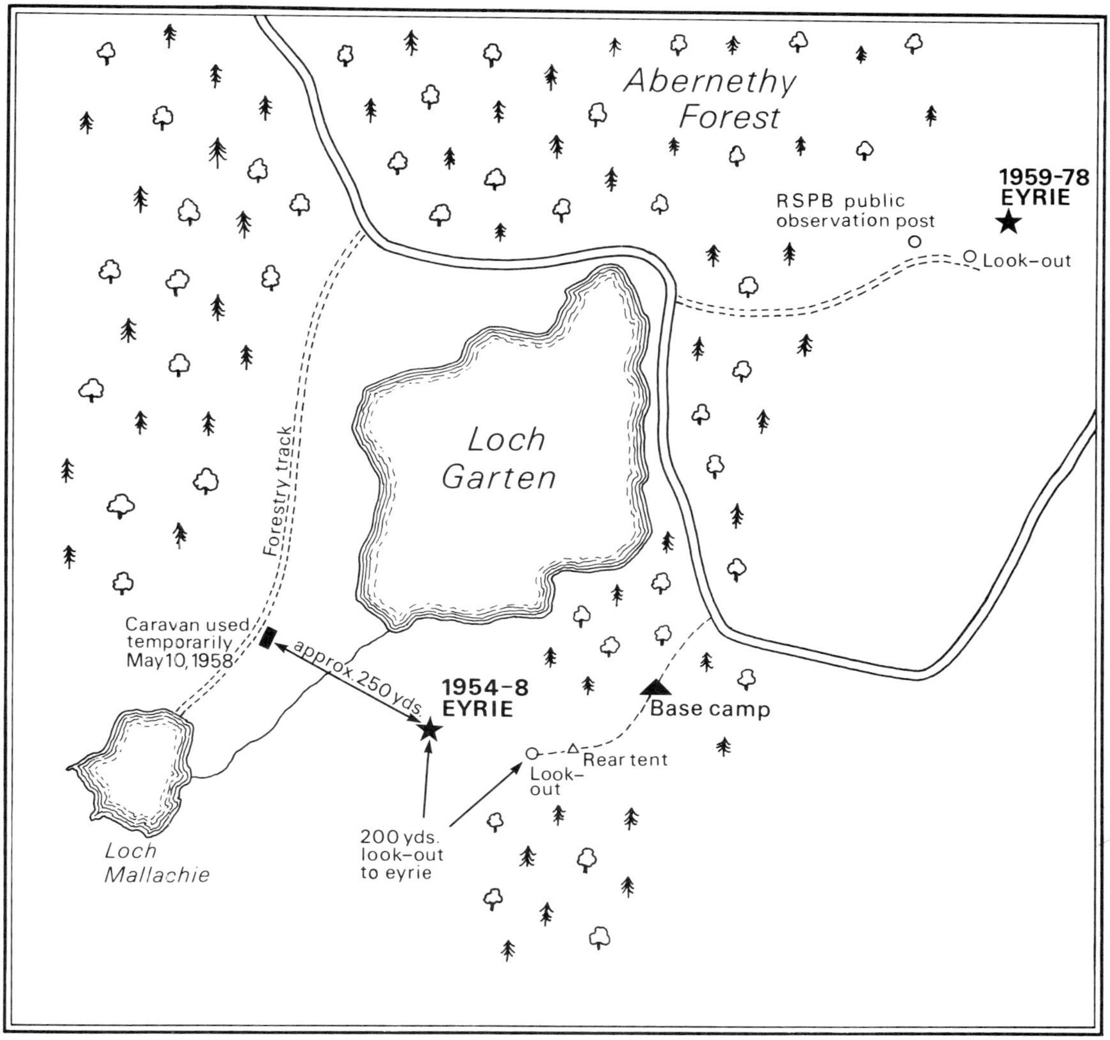

OPERATION OSPREY *in detail*

Author's Note

When the publishers commissioned me to write this book in April 1976, I was under contract to deliver the completed manuscript at the end of that year. Within ten days I was laid low with an attack of shingles on the face and scalp. This started on my right eye; for several months I was deprived of all its usefulness. Late in the autumn of that year, when I was recovering enough to believe (as has turned out to be the case) that my full vision would be restored, I was unexpectedly flattened by a sharpish coronary and not allowed to work for several months. It behoves me to acknowledge the kindness, encouragement and forbearance extended to me by William Heinemann Ltd, during this rather difficult period. I must also warmly thank my Editor, Miss Rosalind Edwards, whose skilful help and unfailing enthusiasm probably saved me from the heinous sin of feeling sorry for myself.

I am also especially grateful to my old friend and colleague, George Waterston, on a number of counts. It was part of my agreement with the publishers that George should write the Foreword and I am delighted that he has done so. Although hundreds of people were involved, one way or another, in Operation Osprey, George was the Supremo. He commanded his limited troops with the utmost skill and dash and drove them ruthlessly on in the cause of his beloved ospreys. I can only hope that I have done justice to his remarkable achievements.

I should also like to thank Christopher Mylne, for his invaluable contribution towards the photographs in this book and, above all, for his patience.

I am grateful to the RSPB, especially to Michael Everett who has supplied me with much useful information. Without the RSPB the ospreys might well not now be breeding in the Scottish Highlands. As deeds are more useful than words I have arranged with my publishers that a substantial proportion of the royalties from the sale of this book shall be paid to the Society.

Philip Brown

Foreword

When I was a small boy, I used to spend much of my spare time in the Bird Room at the Royal Scottish Museum in Edinburgh, enthralled by the range of stuffed birds on display. These were the days when the only really satisfactory bird identification book was T. A. Coward's *Birds of the British Isles*—before the days of 'field guides', colour films and television. Yes, the Museum was the place to learn what things looked like.

Of all the species on view, the birds of prey attracted me most. It was their swashbuckling mode of life and their comparative rarity that appealed. I saw my first buzzard near Loch Morar; they were much scarcer then than today, and I remember photographing my first peregrine eyrie in the Border Hills in 1933. As for golden eagles, my cousin Pat Sandeman and I did what we could to persuade landowners to safeguard these impressive birds in the marginal areas of their range.

But it was the fish-eating osprey which really fired our imaginations. Because it became extinct as a breeding species in Great Britain shortly after the turn of the century, but still appeared occasionally on passage, there was always the hope that some of these Scandinavian migrants might be tempted to nest in the old Highland haunts. Our hopes began to rise when in the 1950s the birds became more and more frequent on migration. Pat was even prompted to erect a cartwheel on a post in Dunalastair Reservoir in the vain hope (as it turned out) of attracting a bird: a method much practised in North America, often with successful results.

Few of the early ornithologists in Scotland were at all interested in conservation. Up to the turn of the twentieth century, most were collectors of skins, eggs and mounted specimens, either for their own private ends or in order to supply museums. The Victorian naturalists were more interested in cataloguing specimens and building up reference collections. Our present knowledge of birds stems from this inheritance.

The Highlands soon became known to a number of wealthy English naturalists, who came north to pillage our rarer Scottish birds—men such as St John, Booth, Wolley and Hancock. Booth shot what was probably the last pair of kites to nest in Speyside.

The osprey is a prime example of a species collected to extinction. As soon as it became scarce, its few remaining eyries were robbed regularly as you will read in this book. Despite efforts made by landowners in its two remaining haunts (in 1893 they were presented with silver medals by the Zoological Society of London to commemorate their efforts), the last of the birds finally ceased to return. I know of only one man still alive today—General Sir Philip Christison—who remembers as a small boy seeing the birds at the old traditional eyrie on Loch an Eilein Castle.

J. A. Harvie-Brown (1844–1916) was really the first person to take an interest in the decline of the ospreys in Scotland. In his series of books on the 'vertebrate faunas' of Scotland, he went to enormous trouble to acquire historical data on the status of the birds. Harvie-Brown's own private collection of skins and eggs was destroyed in a disastrous fire at his home in Dunipace near Larbert in 1897. Fortunately, all his books, journals and correspondence files were saved and are now safely deposited in the library at the Edinburgh office of the Nature Conservancy Council.

I have just recently gone through all this fascinating material. He was a most methodical man; I noted with delight that the list of stores which he and Seebohm were to take to Siberia in 1875 was headed with 'Whisky'! His correspondence with landowners and gamekeepers was voluminous; his efforts to track down information are most impressive. In one file there are numerous copies of catalogues showing bird eggs to be auctioned by Mr J. C. Stevens of London and osprey eggs are featured among them. The bad old days!

In this book, Philip Brown has recaptured the excitements and frustrations we underwent in what can best be described as the 'cloak and dagger' days, when the ospreys returned to nest again after an interval of fifty years. Young wardens today will probably read this book with amazement. In the early days before 'Operation Osprey' was developed into a smooth-running, sophisticated exercise with a comfortable base at Inchdrein, the going was tough. There is little doubt in my mind that the various robberies were very much a matter of a 'dare'—an attempt to thwart the efforts of the Royal Society for the Protection of Birds. The threat of such vandalism makes it all the more important to ensure there's no let-up in the RSPB's vigilance, if the ospreys are to be established as a regular breeding species in Scotland.

The Scottish Ospreys gives us the details of this remarkable saga, its revealing background and its encouraging outcome. Philip, in short, has succeeded in doing full justice to a tale that had to be told.

George Waterston, O.B.E.

CHAPTER ONE

Birds of Prey in General—Ospreys in Particular

The osprey is one of our finest birds of prey. It is the only species (*haliaetus*) in the genus *Pandion* and is found in America, Europe, Asia, Australasia and Africa, although greatly restricted in its range in the last-named continent. The generic name is Greek in origin. Pandion, king of Athens, had two daughters, Philomela and Procne, and according to the legend they all came to an ornithological end. Having married Tereus, king of Thrace, poor Procne found her spouse an inadequate substitute for her sister, whom she loved dearly. In an effort to put matters right, Tereus went off to fetch Philomela so that the sisters could be reunited. Unfortunately, Tereus was pleasantly surprised by Philomela's charms. After seducing her, he subsequently cut out her tongue so as to prevent her telling anyone of his misdeed. On returning from his dramatic mission, Tereus told Procne that her sister was dead.

Truth will out and word eventually reached Procne as to the real state of affairs. In the fine tradition of those old days of olympian blood-and-thunder, Procne murdered her son, Itys, and served up his flesh to Tereus at the next breakfast at which the dumb Philomela unexpectedly appeared as a guest. Tereus was about to destroy the two sisters with his sword when he was suddenly changed into a hoopoe, Procne became a swallow, Itys a pheasant and Philomela a nightingale. One must presume that the gods knew what they were up to and that it was all for the best. They had already changed Pandion into a fish.

The specific name of the osprey, *haliaetus*, is a Greek combination for sea and eagle, but we must not confuse the osprey with any of the several 'sea-eagles' included in the genus *Haliaetus*. In geological time, these 'sea-eagles' have their origins in the Miocene period. They may have been flying twenty million years ago and are among the oldest of raptorial birds, although preceded by some of the owls, a few of the true eagles and some buzzards which date back to Oligocene times, around forty million years ago. The genus *Pandion*, comprising the single species around which this book is written, only evolved less than a million years ago which makes it almost a modern innovation. Even so, it is twice as old as the most primitive form of our own species. Man overshadows all other creatures by virtue of his intelligence, although modern man who indulges in the self-congratulatory exercise of calling himself *Homo sapiens*, has only been in existence for about 30,000 years. The most intelligent, he is also by far the most destructive animal in the brute creation. In very recent times indeed, when not indulging in mass-slaughter on a scale without parallel in history or absorbing earthly resources with careless and selfish abandon that might well contain the seeds of his own self-destruction, this fertile bi-ped—perhaps stricken by his tardy conscience—has set himself up as a conservationist.

Birds of prey, as a group, have attracted man's attention for a long time, not necessarily for their own good. Some definition of what we mean by birds of prey is essential. Many species outside this group are predators: the kingfisher diving to seize an unwary minnow; the swallow hawking for flies; the blackbird pouncing on an earthworm or, in the soft summer gloaming, a nightjar hunting for moths, are just a few examples. Birds of prey, by common usage, include all the diurnal raptorial birds which make up the large and varied Order *Falconiformes* broadly distinguished by their hooked, sharp-pointed bills and powerful feet and talons with which the majority of them seize their prey. Although not closely related to the *Falconiformes*, many ornithologists would include owls as birds of prey. The majority of owls are nocturnal but otherwise their hunting habits are very similar. Owls also possess sharp bills and very strong feet and claws. This is simply because most members of the Order *Strigiformes* hunt and kill their prey in much the same manner as the *Falconiformes,* although they are mostly active at night and have developed a very sharp ear making it possible to home in on their quarry by aural judgement alone; when plunging for the kill the dim shape of their victim looming into view obviously adds to their accuracy.

In this introduction we can forget about the owls—reluctantly, because they are a splendid group of birds—and concentrate our attention on the *Falconiformes* which some purists still regard as the only true birds of prey.

A male osprey 'swearing' at a rival
(Photograph by C. K. Mylne)

There are nearly three hundred different species in this Order of birds. Some are very big: the Andean condor has a wing-span of fully ten feet and weighs well over twenty pounds, avoirdupois. Many are medium-sized, whilst there are plenty of species that are little bigger than a mistle-thrush and a lot that are smaller: a few, such as the falconets in the genus *Microhierax*, are really no bigger than many small passerines.

Their diet is often varied. The monkey-eating eagle of the Philippines also eats birds and even domesticated animals. Some species are almost exclusively carrion-eaters, especially among the vultures and kites, although many species that hunt live prey are also partial to a bit of dead meat, our own common buzzard amongst them. Some species, including the osprey, concentrate on fish, whilst others subsist largely on snakes, lizards and other small reptiles and amphibians.

Some species of birds of prey are wide-ranging, being found almost throughout the world (except Antarctica), whilst others are much restricted in range, sometimes to one relatively small island. Many of the wide-ranging species breed both in the Old World and the New. Golden eagles breed in North America, Europe, Asia and Africa, even if they do have little more than a toe-hold in the latter. Merlins and hen harriers girdle the temperate zone of the Northern Hemisphere, whilst peregrine falcons are almost cosmopolitan. Gyrfalcons are found in the Arctic and cold temperate zones of both the Old and New Worlds, whilst the magnificent white-tailed sea-eagle has a range extending eastwards from Greenland across Europe and Asia, even as far as Japan. Whereas some species seem to be more or less confined to certain climatic zones, others are as much at home in colder regions as they are in the tropics: in the New World the common caracara breeds from California in the north down through Central and South America, even as far as the Falklands, whilst that delighful small falcon of the Old World, the hobby, breeds across northern Europe and in relatively high latitudes in Siberia, as well as in tropical Africa. Many species that breed in high latitudes migrate to warm temperate or tropical zones in the winter months.

While it would be a mistake to suppose that species with a wider breeding range are necessarily common, they are undoubtedly less vulnerable, specifically if not individually, to the growing pressures which man exerts on them in a developing world, compared with those confined to small areas, such as the California condor, the Madagascar serpent eagle, the Seychelles kestrel and the five falconets of the East Indies. In the British Isles, excluding the owls, there are fourteen birds of prey which can be regarded as breeding species:

golden eagle; buzzard; sparrowhawk; goshawk; red kite; honey buzzard; marsh harrier; hen harrier; Montagu's harrier; osprey; hobby; peregrine; merlin and kestrel. The British Isles, in relation to the land surface of the rest of the world, are very small and, on the face of it, this list is not unimpressive, yet only the buzzard, sparrowhawk and kestrel can be regarded as reasonably common. The total nesting pairs of seven of the fourteen species is presently below three figures and in the cases of goshawk, honey buzzard, marsh and Montagu's harrier, and the osprey, the total is below twenty and in single figures, except for the first and last named.

Historically speaking, it might be argued that there has always been a sort of love-hate relationship between man and many birds of prey. Before the arrival of the white man with his somewhat thin veneer of civilization, the Red Indians of North America had such a high regard for eagles that they killed as many as they could to make use of the feathers for their head-dresses: the feathers were regarded as symbols of courage. Falconry is one of the most ancient of British field sports, so that even in mediaeval times strong laws were passed giving protection to certain 'hawks' as well as to some of the species against which the birds were flown, such as the heron. Falconers, in their efforts to obtain young birds to train to the lure, must have made some slight inroads into the numbers of some birds of prey but generally their interests probably did more good than harm—at least until recent times. In Britain today this fine old sport is still practised on a limited scale, although all birds of prey are now given the protection of the law and a person can only take a hawk or falcon under the specific terms of a licence granted by the Nature Conservancy. These licences, quite rightly, are very strictly controlled.

The gradual perfection of the shotgun, coupled with an increasing interest in the shooting of game and wildfowl, had repercussions for birds of prey, including most of the owls, that were sometimes little short of disastrous. Throughout the nineteenth century, and into the present one, large estates flourished. A very small minority enjoyed what, by modern standards, would be regarded as a great deal of wealth, and labour was cheap. Even small sporting estates employed a keeper and one or two underkeepers, while some of the larger ones were bristling with these tough, hard-working men who were bred to regard as 'vermin' anything that might be in any way detrimental to their job of producing a good head of game. So they waged constant war against a good many species of animals and birds with the aid of guns, traps and poison. Shepherds, especially in hill country, also regarded some of the larger birds of prey—as well as foxes and badgers—not always unreasonably as a threat to the safety of their charges on which, like the keepers, their rather meagre livelihoods depended. Many modern conservationists are probably not unmindful of their pay packets.

In the first section of this book I record in greater detail the ruthless manner in which some birds of prey were slaughtered. However, this wholly unnatural pressure did not come solely from those who were ready to sacrifice almost any living creature in what they believed to be the best interests of game preservation. Collectors, whether of skins or eggs, plundered and looted on a preposterous scale. The rarer a species, the more attractive it became. If some birds—the osprey among them—were let off comparatively lightly by the sporting interests because they were not considered likely to do much damage, the collectors stopped at nothing; as a class, too, they were usually intelligent and even cultured men who, unlike most keepers, must have been aware of the adverse effects their activities were bound to have on the birds that clearly interested them very much and which many of them professed to cherish and admire.

Fishermen, too, have always been prone to raise objection to anything that might be seen to interfere with their good sport. Some animals, such as otters, ospreys and even kingfishers, have been persecuted to this end. It would be wrong, however, to conclude that the adverse pressures on wildlife were much greater in the nineteenth century than they have so far been during the twentieth. The wilderness has been in retreat for a long time, but this process has never been so rapid, nor its effects more startling, than during the last hundred years. There are so many relevant factors, some peculiar to particular countries or districts, that it would be impossible even to attempt to list them all. The effects of the Industrial Revolution and the endless growth of urbanization are simply two of several more obvious ones. Efficient agriculture, drainage, dredging of streams and rivers and the clearing of banks, afforestation and tree-felling, mineral extraction and the provision of recreational activities are among the others. These things have wrought great changes in the fauna and flora of large areas yet must not all be assumed to have been detrimental to wildlife. In Britain, the proliferation of disused gravel-pits, for example, has undoubtedly been beneficial for the populations of some duck and other water birds. However, if these new stretches of inland water are given over to speed-boating, sailing, fishing or some other similar activity, then they are largely rendered useless for many species of birds, at any rate in the nesting season, when reasonable peace and quiet are often essential ingredients for the successful rearing of young. Within this book I can do no more than indicate that the conservation of wildlife is both a complex and difficult business.

* * *

The osprey is among the larger of raptorial birds: in Britain it is second only to the golden eagle, being approximately the size of a goshawk, a species with broader, shorter wings but a bulkier body. The osprey has a wing-span of fully five feet, yet it often looks rather slow in flight, but always strong and purposeful and it can move much faster when circumstances demand, as when chasing a crow or buzzard which has approached close to its eyrie. Head and neck are predominantly white with a few dark streaks on the crown and a broad, blackish eye-stripe. Apart from a band of brown streaks on the upper breast, the underparts are pure white in striking contrast with the dark brown, almost blackish upperparts: viewed from any distance, it looks like a big black-and-white bird. In flight the wings often look crooked. The tail is only of moderate length, perhaps rather narrow in relation to the size of the rest of the bird. Ospreys in North America show little of the streaking on the breast, while those in south-east Asia and Australia have whiter heads.

The deliberate persecution of many raptorial species has not been a peculiarly British phenomenon. Thus Arthur Bent, one of the many outstanding American ornithologists, in his *Life Histories of North American Birds of Prey*, written only a few years before the outbreak of the Second World War, had this to say about the osprey's human enemies: 'the thoughtless gunner, who shoots every large bird that he can, and the greedy egg-collector, who takes all the eggs he can get for exchange . . .' Yet all the blame for the wanton destruction of many kinds of birds of prey in what are regarded as highly civilized countries does not rest, by any means, only on the shoulders of the trigger-happy shooters and kleptomaniacal egg-collectors. The interest in owning and flying racing pigeons is widespread in many countries, including Great Britain. Some of these pigeons, from a commercial aspect, are very valuable. Sooner or later a fair number of birds fail to make their home-lofts after being raced and are posted as 'missing, believed dead'. Many of these casualties are caused by natural circumstances, especially by adverse winds and stormy weather, but a handful certainly fall victim to birds of prey, principally the peregrine falcon. However, I believe it fair to say that many organizations concerned with this sport which is enjoyed by millions and often detested by their immediate neighbours, have often kicked up a hullabaloo about predatory birds which is out of all proportion to the known facts. The damage that has been done to some birds of prey during this century makes incredible reading. Thus, at least until fairly recently, the Belgian Federation of Pigeon-Fanciers apparently paid substantial monetary rewards for two complete legs from a red kite, sparrowhawk, peregrine and goshawk, among others; in the late 1950s the annual toll averaged over 7,000 birds.

In Belgium, ospreys were destroyed because of damage they were alleged to do on trout hatcheries; only when they had been exterminated as a nesting species were they afforded legal protection in 1963—another crass example of securing the stable door after the horse has bolted. However, the greatest disaster that has probably ever overtaken birds of prey (as well as many other animals, too) lay in the hasty and promiscuous use of certain highly toxic and persistent chemicals. The literature on this subject is extensive but in this introduction I must reluctantly deal with it rather briefly.

Spreading its powerful wings, an osprey lands on its eyrie
(Photograph by C. K. Mylne)

This particular tragedy started after the conclusion of the Second World War and its most serious effects, insofar as wildlife was concerned, were felt in the 1950s and 60s. Our American friends, if they were first in the field in using these toxics, were certainly first in sounding the alarm. A typical example dates from 1954. DDT was employed in ever-increasing quantities to control certain pests. Early in the 1950s this persistent compound featured in an extensive spraying campaign undertaken in the United States in an attempt to eradicate the beetle causing Dutch elm disease. I now quote from my own book—*Birds of Prey* (André Deutsch, London, 1964):

'. . . it so happened that in 1954 two ornithologists, Professor Wallace and one of his students at Michigan State University, started work in the university campus on the population of robins. This was, of course, the American robin which is really a thrush with a brick-red breast. At the same time, purely by coincidence, a programme of spraying for Dutch elm disease was started in the same area. In this first year the spraying was light and no untoward effects were noted among the robins, which are migratory birds moving south from their breeding grounds in autumn and returning in spring.

'In 1955 the spraying programme was stepped up and the effect on the robins was at once obvious. Almost as soon as the first birds returned, numbers were picked up dead and dying as each new wave of migrants flew in from the south, so there would be a fresh outbreak of sick birds and corpses. Nesting activities were few and the number of young robins reared even fewer. Gradually the causes came to light. The elm trees were usually sprayed in the spring and often again in the summer. Inevitably much of the DDT went on to the ground and so into the soil, for it is characteristic of the chlorinated hydrocarbons that they persist for a very long time—often for years.

'The earthworm feeding on rotting leaves and other vegetable food inevitably ingested varying amounts of DDT and because they provided the main food of the robin, the poison got into the birds. The worms, of course, were only carrying sub-lethal doses, but the robins could be expected to eat many worms in a day. In a few years the robin population was more than decimated. It was estimated that there were 370 adults in the study areas prior to the spraying programme and that these could normally be expected to produce at least their own number in fledged young, yet in 1957 only one young robin was seen and the following year

Dr Wallace said that neither he, nor anybody else, had seen a single fledgling.'

Rachel Carson in her remarkable book *Silent Spring* cites many other examples, including the catastrophe that overtook the Western grebe population on Clear Lake, California. This water was infested with a small species of gnat and the authorities decided to spray with DDD, another chlorinated hydrocarbon closely related to DDT but considered to be less harmful to the fish. This insecticide was applied in what was considered to be a safe solution: in fact so weak that there was only one part of DDD to seventy million parts of water. This was done in 1949 and the gnats were brought under control for a time. However, five years later the gnats were back in force. Another spraying programme was planned and it was decided to increase the strength of the dose. Even so, the dilution was considered safe enough: only one part of DDD to fifty million parts of water. The result appeared satisfactory, the elimination of the gnats seemingly complete. Yet the following winter the unexpected, uncalculated side-effects began to show themselves. The grebes which fed on the fish in the lake began to die in considerable numbers. Annoyingly enough, the remnant of the gnat population soon staged a remarkable recovery. Three years later, in 1957, yet a third spraying was carried out and this was followed by much greater mortality amongst the grebes. On analysing the corpses it was discovered that they carried high concentrations of DDD. The strongest spray applied to the water was only one-fiftieth of a part per million, yet in some of the dead birds it was as high as 1,600 parts per million. The grebes had eaten the fish that, in turn, had been feeding on smaller aquatic life and as DDD was also a highly persistent compound, the lethal effects had been passed up the natural food chain, accumulating within the grebes until it killed them.

Predatory birds, among other animals, were also at the end of a food chain. It was not long before the seriousness of the situation on both sides of the Atlantic became obvious. It was not simply that the accumulation of the chlorinated hydrocarbons built up in the body fats of the birds until it finally poisoned many of them; it was soon discovered that adults which survived often lost their fertility. Thus in 1961 no less than 253 nesting sites of the peregrine falcon were visited in England, Wales and southern Scotland. Many of these sites were unoccupied and only 22 pairs of peregrines succeeded in rearing any young at all. The population crashed so fast that within a year or two it was feared that the species might even become extinct in Britain. By then, however, the public outcry, spearheaded by the Royal Society for the

Protection of Birds and well supported by press and radio, had compelled the government to take action. It was all very fine to talk about increasing the food supply by using substances as lethal as dieldrin and endrin, yet it began to be appreciated that man, too, was at the end of a food chain and that unless some commonsense prevailed, there might soon be fewer human mouths to feed! By the mid-1960s in Great Britain, the majority of the most persistent and lethal compounds had been dropped, yet even now, almost fifteen years later, many of those birds and other animals (the otter is a good example) have still neither recovered their former numbers nor, in some cases, their ability to reproduce.

British ospreys escaped the worst effects of these persistent chemicals for several reasons. This promiscuous use was more or less confined to the ten years, 1956 till 1965. During most of that time, so far as we know, only one pair of ospreys was attempting to breed in Britain, except towards the end of the period when a second pair was found. Again, the area of the Scottish Highlands was one where the use of the most lethal chemicals was minimal. In North America, on the other hand, the osprey situation was much more depressing. Thus in one area in Connecticut where about 150 pairs had been nesting in 1954, ten years later this had been reduced to 15. Some of the females did not lay any eggs at all, while those that did tended to produce smaller clutches than usual and many eggs failed to hatch. Some of these infertile eggs were taken for subsequent analysis. They contained large amounts of DDT and derivatives, as did remains of fish picked up around the nests. It was not simply that, in the space of ten years or less, the numbers of some species of raptors were reduced by eighty or ninety per cent: many of those remaining were incapable of breeding.

The osprey must for a very long time have been one of the more familiar birds of prey in the United States of America. A. C. Bent, in the 1930s, wrote:

> 'In a few favourable localities, mainly along the Atlantic coast, it is very abundant and breeds in several more or less dense colonies. As it lives entirely on fish, it naturally prefers to live in the vicinity of the sea coast or near some large body of water, lake or stream. Given this food supply, it makes little difference to the osprey what its surroundings are. It is equally at home near the shore of some remote wilderness lake, on timbered or open islands along the coast, in the valleys of inland streams, in open farming country, or even close to houses. In the last two localities it is jealously protected and often encouraged to breed by placing cart-

Erecting an old cart-wheel to attract ospreys in Abernethy Forest
(Photograph by C. K. Mylne)

wheels or other supports for its nest in trees or on poles. In the region where I am most familiar with it, it has become a common dooryard bird, almost a domestic pet, and consequently very tame.'

Some of the 'colonies' of ospreys must have been very impressive. The late Capt. C. W. R. Knight was on Gardiner's Island (off Long Island, New York) in 1932 and estimated that over 300 pairs were breeding in an area of about 3,000 acres. This gives a density of over 50 pairs breeding to a square mile. Those were the great days for American ospreys and perhaps nothing quite like it will ever be seen again. In Europe ospreys are generally regarded as somewhat solitary in their nesting habits, but this might partly be due to circumstances. In the early 1930s there were almost certainly more pairs of ospreys breeding in that one colony on Gardiner's Island than in the whole of north-west Europe. However, in some places in Germany ospreys are said to breed within a mile of one another, which is more akin to colonial nesting than anything found in Scandinavia, let alone the Highlands of Scotland where, to our knowledge, a total population of around twenty pairs is spread over six or seven counties.

The global distribution of the osprey is remarkably wide. However, within this range the numbers present vary greatly. In some instances the paucity of breeding birds or, sometimes, the fact that they are no longer present at all, may be attributed to deliberate persecution by man. The Mediterranean basin is probably as good an example of how the species has been greatly reduced in numbers, whilst Scotland during the nineteenth century offers a classic demonstration of just how a healthy and generally harmless population of ospreys can be completely wiped out through the ruthless stupidity and greed of those who were otherwise frequently very agreeable persons.

In North America, although the breeding range of the osprey stretches in a broad band from east to west, the majority of birds are concentrated towards the eastern seaboard. Almost wholly dependent on fish for food, the osprey when nesting must have a reasonable source of supply within easy distance. In the higher latitudes of the north, where the birds can do well for themselves in the warmer summer months, they have to migrate south in autumn to avoid the rigours of winter—while those breeding in warm temperate and tropical areas are much more sedentary.

In the two sections that follow we shall trace the earlier history of the osprey in Scotland, followed by the adventures and misadventures that finally led to their re-establishment as a British breeding species. Before closing this introduction, however, a brief account of the breeding biology of our subject may assist the reader to understand better all that follows.

Scottish ospreys, like those in Scandinavia, migrate south in autumn. This autumn migration appears to be a fairly leisurely business. Birds that have successfully reared young during the previous summer are more or less free of family ties towards the very end of August or early September. Although it is probable that ospreys may pair for life, the family bond disintegrates with the onset of autumn and there is no sound evidence to suggest that even the birds that form the pair keep together for long once they have left the breeding grounds, let alone the young. Throughout September and October ospreys are often seen fishing in suitable waters in England, Wales and southern Scotland, more frequently on the eastern side than the west. It must not be presumed that all these travellers are Scottish birds, because many of them are likely to have come from Norway and Sweden rather than Scotland. Partly due to protective legislation, but mainly to public interest and goodwill, the number of ospreys breeding in Norway and Sweden has considerably increased since the Second World War, more especially over the last ten or fifteen years. If it can never be proven, it is probable that it was this small but regular and increasing passage through England and Scotland of birds of Scandinavian origin which eventually led to the initial establishment of some of the Scottish pairs.

The first birds return to the Scottish Highlands when, more often than not, the weather is still more characteristic of winter than spring. Usually, not invariably, the cock bird is the first to put in an appearance at the old eyrie, rarely before March is out, most frequently in April, occasionally not until May. The second bird of the pair normally joins the first within a week or ten days.

On arrival at the eyrie in early spring a cock will spend a varying amount of time in and around the nest, sometimes disappearing for hours, even occasionally for a day or two. He will fiddle about on the eyrie and sometimes bring in a small stick or some other bit of building material. Once the female has joined him things often start to move very fast indeed. The period of courtship generally lasts for about a week or ten days, sometimes even less. Refurbishing the old nest is undertaken without delay. Whilst both sexes will collect this building material, the major part is undertaken by the male, but the female spends more time arranging and fitting it into the structure. When building or rebuilding a nest, an osprey will bring in enormous sticks, mostly if not entirely dead matter, up to fully three feet in length and over an

A female osprey bringing in an enormous stick
(Photograph by Joe Van Wormer/Bruce Coleman Limited)

inch in thickness. Some of these sticks are picked up from the ground, but many others are dead boughs snapped off trees, the bird swooping down on the branch, seizing it with his talons and, with luck, breaking it off with a crack that, in any quiet place, sounds as loud as a pistol shot. Apart from these sticks, which really form the basis of the whole structure, tough grasses, lumps of moss, and long twigs of heather are gathered and incorporated; moss, heather and grass being much favoured at the expense of sticks when the work is nearing completion and the female is lining the often large but relatively shallow 'cup'. The number of items brought into the eyrie may vary from as little as a hundred or two to much nearer a thousand. If in a somewhat desultory way, the gathering of nesting material continues whilst the female is laying her clutch of eggs and, indeed, even later; lumps of moss and heather may be collected long after the chicks have hatched out.

During the most intensive period of building the male often displays above the eyrie, calling noisily as he flies a few hundred feet up and then diving down to the nest on which his mate is probably standing. This dramatic display-flighting, as with nest building, is carried on most frequently during the forenoon.

Mating takes place on the eyrie itself, the female soliciting the male by adopting a crouching attitude, raising her tail and fanning her wings. Copulation is brief, but may take place half a dozen or more times in the course of the day—and continue, with decreasing frequency, for a few days after the hen has completed her clutch.

The time elapsing between the arrival of the first bird at the eyrie and the laying of the first egg is highly variable, but may be reckoned around three weeks. Normally a hen lays a clutch of two or three eggs, rarely four, and sometimes only one. It has been suggested that the usual interval between the laying of one egg and the next is approximately 48 hours, but in fact the intervals are often irregular. Thus the second egg in a clutch of three may be laid the day after the first, then two days pass before the laying of the last one. This is a matter of considerable interest but not of any great moment to the success or otherwise of the breeding cycle.

Incubation follows very soon after the laying of the first egg. Almost invariably the female sits throughout the night following the day she produced her first egg, but she may sit all night on the nest prior to the morning when she lays her first egg. Unless the nest can be inspected (which is usually impossible without causing the birds unnecessary and undesirable disturbance) it is sometimes difficult to decide on what date the first egg is laid. Both sexes share in the task of incubation, although the female certainly undertakes by far the larger share, invariably responsible for the longish 'night-shift'. Change-overs occur at irregular intervals, varying from a few minutes up to several hours: if the male is away fishing the female can do nothing but sit and await his return although sometimes, as if she were losing her patience, she will give voice to a series of peevish-sounding notes.

The incubation period for our Scottish ospreys is in the order of 37 or 38 days. Most Scottish-born ospreys probably hatch out during the first fortnight in June. During incubation the male catches and brings back about two fish a day, occasionally three or four but sometimes only one. Pike and trout feature largely in the diet, roughly in about equal proportions. Many of these fish are fairly small, below a pound in weight; a three pounder is exceptional and when an osprey, having climbed up from the river or loch several miles away with this weight held in his talons, approaches the eyrie, he is often visibly tiring, flying fairly low over the ground and circling two or three times in order to gain sufficient height to come into the eyrie and present it to the female, who will immediately fly off with it to a nearby perch leaving her mate to keep the eggs warm. In fact, during the five long weeks of incubation, the cock often lands on a nearby perch and eats his fill before presenting what is left to the hen. One of the significant behavioural changes which coincides with the hatch is that the male thenceforth almost always takes the prey straight to the nest, retiring fishless to a perch, waiting patiently until the female has fed the chicks, had her own share and resettled to brood before flying up to the eyrie, grabbing the remains of the fish and returning to his perch to eat it.

Once the chicks have hatched out the male has to step up his hunting, bringing in four or five fish each day. The fledging period is a long and very active one, when anyone watching the eyrie will experience few dull moments. For the first five or six weeks the female tears off the flesh from the prey and carefully feeds her young, morsel by morsel, but thereafter the chicks start to get at the fish for themselves in a boisterous free-for-all. By now the fledglings are well-grown and well-plumaged, spending more and more of their time wobbling around the rim of the eyrie and indulging in vigorous wing-flapping exercises. Near the end of the eighth week after hatching, the strongest youngster is likely to launch out on his first flight—the others soon following his example. For several days, though, the chicks return to the eyrie late in the evening, staying there until after sunrise. Then the nest is more or less abandoned for the season, adults and young roosting overnight on branches, preferably dead, in nearby trees. If all has gone well, the chicks will make their first, tentative

The latest fish being devoured eagerly on a nearby perch
(Photograph by L. R. Dawson/Bruce Coleman Limited)

flights towards the end of July or early in August. About a fortnight later they will be moving out of the nesting area, although it may be possible to discover them learning the arts of fishing in the company of their parents late in August and during the first half of September.

However briefly, I hope I have succeeded in giving the reader enough basic information about the breeding cycle of the osprey to enable him the better to enjoy what follows. If all goes well, the breeding cycle is a long one, one or more ospreys being present at the eyrie for well over four months and the family remaining in the vicinity a further three or four weeks. Twenty-four weeks is a fair chunk out of any year and for much of that time the adult ospreys will have been tied to the eyrie and have had to work hard to provide for their family. One gets attached to these magnificent birds between which the family bond is quite close-knit while it lasts. If it seems sad when, inevitably, the birds start on their leisurely autumnal journey southwards to enjoy a spell of warmth and perhaps a bit of avian 'lotus-eating' in Africa, it would seem churlish to begrudge them this reward for their labours.

Nowadays when the ospreys leave their nesting grounds in autumn, one can confidently anticipate their return in the following spring. It is as well to remember that it was not always thus. Our forefathers drove the ospreys out of Britain, mostly leaving their grandsons and great-grandsons to hang their heads in shame. Even twenty years ago, when a pair of ospreys was still struggling to get a toe-hold in the Highlands, there was never any certainty that they would come back in the spring. For those of us who enjoyed the rare privilege of trying to cushion the birds against the impact of egg thieves and other dangers, disaster always seemed to be looming round the next corner—and, all too often, it was.

CHAPTER TWO

Extirpation of Ospreys in Scotland

The history of ospreys in the British Isles, especially outside Scotland, is comparatively little known. This is really rather astonishing, bearing in mind the size of the bird and its relative conspicuousness. It surely must have been tolerably familiar if it was ever widespread as a breeding species in Great Britain, yet there is no really satisfactory evidence that ospreys ever nested in Ireland, an island in which there must always have been plenty of highly suitable habitat. In the third volume of Witherby's *The Handbook of British Birds*, first published in 1939 and which has remained the most comprehensive and authoritative work of its kind for almost forty years, the species is not credited as ever having nested outside Scotland anywhere in the British Isles. I quote:

> 'Distribution—British Isles. Rare but regular passage-migrant. Formerly summer resident in a good many places in Scotland, but now extinct as breeding species. Last bred at Loch Arkaig in 1908 and single bird there until 1913; last bred at Loch an Eilean in 1899 and in 1901 and 1902 only a single bird, after these dates both these localities forsaken. There is evidence of breeding at Loch Luichart and elsewhere on occasions since this, but we have not definite proof of this. In England, regular but rare passage-migrant (September-October and March-May, fairly often July-August, sometimes June, occasionally November) occurring every year on some part of coast or on inland waters, but most regularly Norfolk; migrants also recorded occasionally in Scotland and several times in last ten years in summer. Rarely Wales, only once O. Hebrides, and very rarely Orkney, and Ireland (last Co. Down, 1929).'

In our book, *The Return of the Osprey*, published in 1962 by Collins, George Waterston discussed what little past evidence was available and drew the conclusion that ospreys must have bred, at least in some parts of England, in past centuries, yet some of the records are unsatisfactory and relatively few wholly convincing. It seems likely that the osprey was sometimes confused with the white-tailed sea-eagle—a much larger bird—and vice-versa. The decline in the fortunes of the sea-eagle probably began late in the eighteenth century and the bird was extinct as a breeding species by the end of the first decade of the twentieth. At any rate, the nesting habitats of sea-eagle and osprey must have overlapped, to some extent, in those parts of Britain where they both occurred. Whereas the osprey feeds almost wholly on fish, the diet of the sea-eagle is much more varied, including many mammals and birds as large as the heron and curlew. Whilst it nested on sea cliffs, the sea-eagle also bred on rocky islands in lochs, much as the osprey often did, so that it cannot be regarded as altogether surprising if confusion occurred in times when observers were generally far less critical than their modern counterparts. Nevertheless, the balance of the evidence, for what it is worth, does suggest that ospreys nested in some districts of England a century and more ago, particularly in Devonshire where the habitat, especially on Exmoor, might well have been suitable, and also in the Lake District in what is now the county of Cumbria. I am fairly familiar with the old counties of Cumberland and Westmorland and, if ever the ospreys return to breed south of the Border it strikes me that there are areas in the English Lakes which would suit them admirably, perhaps more so than ever now that some much-maligned re-afforestation is growing towards maturity. There is no satisfactory evidence to suggest that ospreys ever bred in Wales, although some of the terrain in that lovely country would surely have been suitable enough. Even in England, within historical times, it was almost certainly uncommon as a breeding species except, perhaps, in one or two favoured localities.

The osprey has always been associated with Scotland and it is, typically, a bird of the Highlands from where it was driven into temporary exile through the greed and the follies of men. There is no point in blinking the facts: the gradual perfection of the shotgun and the development of game shooting was one of the worst disasters that has ever overtaken our birds of prey. It is customary to put the blame on generations of gamekeepers, yet it should be remembered that, at least until fairly recently, employers told their workmen what they should and should not do. Apart from the fact that even absentee landlords cannot escape their share of the blame, many of the landowners did not fall into that category. As grouse shooting grew in importance so birds of prey fell out of favour.

We must, however, be careful not to apply twentieth-century standards to things which occurred a hundred and more years ago. We must also remember that in those far-off days natural history was still in its infancy, ecology had never been heard of and knowledge of wild birds and beasts and their inter-relationships between themselves and their environment was no more than embryonic. Enjoying the benefit of hindsight it is obvious that many things that happened were disastrous and no doubt a good deal of selfishness and even stupidity—fairly common human attributes—were involved. Yet in trying to arrive at any kind of objective assessment, it should be appreciated that the hysterical and the historical are bad mixers if we are seeking the truth.

Long before the middle of the nineteenth century the pressure was being applied to almost every bird of prey in the Highlands. Such records as we have make grisly reading. In his book, *Days with the Golden Eagle*, Seton Gordon cited the example of 98 golden eagles destroyed in the two years 1839–40, on the Glen Garry estate alone. If we accept these figures, coming from only one estate, then even if the golden eagle population was considerably higher at that time than it is today (and it almost certainly was) the chief reason for the decline in the species is obvious. Eighteen ospreys were recorded as destroyed on the same estate over a similar period. Elsewhere in the Highlands the situation was just as bad, if not worse. On one estate in Sutherland, during the course of only three years in the early 1830s, A. J. Selby published a list of 'vermin' destroyed, including 171 adult golden eagles, 53 young eagles or eggs and over 1,000 unspecified hawks, although he added that ospreys 'remain generally unmolested by the hunters, as they never attack lambs'. It is unlikely that ospreys did go 'unmolested'. Even if they were not destroyed by keepers to any large extent, they were already rare in many areas and uncommon in others and were eagerly sought after by skin and egg collectors willing to pay, by the low living standards of the native highlanders, temptingly high prices. The books of Charles St John, all of them readable classics of their kind, provide a remarkable insight into what was going on around the middle of the nineteenth century.

Whilst his name will always be associated with the Highlands and its natural history, Charles St John was a Sassenach. He was born at Chailey, in Sussex, in 1809 and went to school at Midhurst. Even as a boy he was a proficient angler, spinning for pike and eels in the Arun. At the age of 19 he was working in the Treasury but found office life irksome. Relief soon came; his uncle, Lord Bolingbroke, lent him a shooting lodge in Sutherland, Rosehall, where he devoted himself to a life of sport and observation of many wild creatures. In 1834, at the age of twenty-five, he married the daughter of a Newcastle banker, inheriting a small fortune as one result. He moved to Morayshire, but in 1853 was seized by a stroke whilst out shooting. Brought back to the south of England under the mistaken notion that the climate of Hampshire was more beneficial than that of Moray, he died at Woolstone in 1856 at the early age of 47. Yet he packed more adventure into his short life than most people who live twice as long.

One of St John's best books is his *Tour in Sutherlandshire*, first published in 1849, in which he describes how, in the spring of 1848, he set out on 'an excursion through some part of the county of Sutherland, which I shall endeavour to describe, in the hope of inducing others to follow my example, confident that whoever does so will find himself amply repaid for his trouble'. His preparations for this expedition into some of the wildest and most forbidding

Cock osprey in flight over a well-grown chick
(Photograph by C. K. Mylne)

country in the kingdom, where roads were few and mostly very bad, are obvious from his own account:

> 'Our start from Bonar Bridge was a most amusing affair, not only to ourselves but also to all the inhabitants of that small but beautifully situated village. The vehicle which we travelled in was a small and lightly built flat-bottomed boat, made of larch, and mounted on wheels. It was constructed to ship and unship in half a minute. By simply unscrewing two bolts, it could be taken off its wheels and launched into the water. Being on springs, it made a very easy carriage, and was large enough to hold four persons, with plenty of room for baggage. On the present occasion our party consisted of a friend of mine, Mr J., who (although for many years a wanderer over Switzerland and many parts of Europe) had never been through the wilder and more mountainous regions of Scotland: Mr Dunbar (William, the brother of Lewis Dunbar of whom we shall hear more later), whose assistance was of much use as a naturalist and interpreter amongst the shepherds and others who spoke more Gaelic than English; myself, and Leo, my retriever.
>
> 'Having adjusted the harness, traces, etc., of the boat to my horse (a stout Highland 'garron'), we started at an early hour, trusting to the chapter of accidents and the pace of our horse as to where we should sleep that night, but determined to make out as many miles as we could, or in other words to advance as far as possible into the mountainous parts of Sutherlandshire. Bonar Bridge is situated on what is called the Kyle of Sutherland . . . In winter this water abounds with wild fowl, but now (May 14) all these birds have gone to their breeding places with the exception of a solitary godwit or two, who seem to have been left behind the rest of their comrades, this bird not breeding in Scotland. The woods above Rosehall, or rather that portion of them which the axe has spared, used to abound in many kinds of interesting hawks, and also in marten and wild cats, but keepers and trapping combined seem to have entirely swept all these animals away. I looked in vain for buzzards on a high rock which some years back was invariably tenanted by them, but it seemed that they had long since been destoyed.'

Charles St John, with the ready and stout assistance of William Dunbar, did a fair amount of collecting for museums, notably for James Hancock, some of whose booty can still be enjoyed by visitors to the Hancock Museum at Barras Bridge, in Newcastle-upon-Tyne. A dead bird, or skin, or a clutch of blown eggs are of scant interest to posterity in comparison with the sight of some fine bird alive, wild and free, but the amassing of some of these early collections was by no means founded on sheer selfishness and they contributed considerably to our knowledge of ornithology. However, if St John could justly claim that: 'Not being a collector of eggs or birds myself, I had no wish to destroy more of my feathered friends than sufficed to prove their identity, and to procure a few specimens for a gentleman who is as great a lover of nature as myself, and a far more scientific one,' it is difficult to excuse the ruthlessness of some of his executions. On the other hand, reading his books, one is compelled to admire his enthusiasm, determination and fortitude. His ability as a naturalist was unquestionably high and his interest in natural history both deep and genuine.

This is St John's account of an encounter with that attractive small wader, the red-necked phalarope on the edge of Loch Naver:

> 'In the swampy ground near the west end of the lake a vast number of birds seem to breed. Snipes, curlews, redshanks, plovers etc., etc., all keep up a constant cry of alarm on any intrusion into their dominion. While I was fishing, Mr Dunbar called my attention to two beautiful little birds near the edge of the water, which he pronounced to be the red-necked phalarope. Not having any specimens in his collection, he went to the inn for a gun, while I sat down to watch them. The red-necked phalarope is certainly the most beautiful little wader of my acquaintance. There were a pair of them, male and female, feeding near the loch, in a little pool which was covered with weeds of different kinds. Nothing could be more graceful than the movements of these two little birds as they swam about in search of insects, etc. Sometimes they ran lightly on the broad leaves of the water-lily, which served them for a raft and entirely kept them out of the water . . . They seemed to have not the slightest fear of me, for frequently they came within a yard of where I was sitting, and, after looking up, they continued catching the small water-insects, etc., on the weeds without minding my presence in the least.'

Phalaropes are notoriously tame but the trust of these particular birds was clearly misplaced:

> 'After having apparently exhausted the food in one pool, on a signal from the male they suddenly both took wing, and flew away to a fresh feeding-place two or three hundred yards off, where we afterwards found

Three richly marked ospreys' eggs in an eyrie
(Photograph by Jen and Des Bartlett/Bruce Coleman Limited)

them. Though we could not discover their nest, I have no doubt that they had eggs very near the spot where we saw them. Indeed, on dissecting the female (Dunbar had obtained his gun all right) we found two eggs in her, nearly full-sized, so that probably she had already deposited the other two, which would have made her number complete. I find no account of this bird breeding on the mainland of Scotland.'

Given the sort of reception afforded them by St John and Dunbar, this was, perhaps, scarcely surprising. On the green islands in Loch Meadie (Maddie), earlier on the tour, the party had found greylag geese nesting and St John wrote: 'To make sure of the species I shot some of the old birds, it having been rather a disputed question among several of my friends as to whether the goose breeding in this country is the Greylag or the Bean goose.'

Sea-eagles were persecuted by shepherds and egg-collectors, yet even in the middle of the nineteenth century they were probably still fairly numerous in the Highlands and some of the more suitable Scottish islands. However, confusion certainly occurred between this species and the golden eagle and few keepers were likely to give any bird of prey the benefit of the doubt. Once grouse shooting really came into vogue almost all birds of prey were ruthlessly harried, anyway.

St John gives the status of all the species he encountered on this tour of Sutherland. He described the sea-eagle as 'perhaps more numerous than the golden eagle; living, as it does, principally in the lofty cliffs of the sea coast, and feeding more on dead fish and food found on the shore, it does not so often fall in the war of the trapper or fox-hunter: it breeds, sometimes, among the inland mountains.'

As to the status of the golden eagle in Sutherland, St John summed it up thus, '(It) is still to be found tolerably numerous, but gradually decreasing, in the north and north-west part of the country; though likely to be soon extirpated, owing to game-preserving and sheep-farming. To the latter the eagle is far more destructive than to the former.'

If shepherds might have agreed with that last remark, it seems highly probable that few, if any, contemporary keepers would have done so. In spite of incessant persecution by keepers, shepherds and collectors, the golden eagle has never been completely extirpated from Sutherland, although this was not due to any fault of St John and his friends:

> 'Between Loch Laighal (Loyal) and Tongue, on driving round the corner of a rock, we suddenly came upon two golden eagles who were hunting close to the ground. They were nearly within shot of us; so, leaving the horse and carriage to take care of themselves, we jumped out, gun in hand, to try to get shots at them. Two or three times the birds swooped down, and one of them carried off some bird, probably a grouse, taking it far away round the cliffs of Ben Laighal. The other eagle then made a sudden swoop down to the ground, within a hundred yards of us, but just behind a small hillock; we ran to the place, confident of getting the bird, but arrived just in time to see the eagle carrying off its prey, whatever it was, in the same direction as that taken by its mate, in all probability straight to the nest.'

St John's admiration for eagles and ospreys was genuine enough, yet one wonders if it ever occurred to him that, had he shot one of those eagles at Loch Loyal, one or more young eaglets might have perished in their eyrie?

St John once wrote of the golden eagle that 'it should be rather preserved than exterminated', but in his *Wild Sports and Natural History of the Highlands*, first published in 1846, he gives a vivid description of an occasion when, out shooting ptarmigan with a keeper:

> 'a magnificent eagle suddenly rose almost at our feet, as we came to the edge of a precipice, on a shelf of which, near the summit, he had been resting. Bang went one barrel at him at a distance of twenty yards. The small shot struck him severely, and, drooping his legs, he rose in the air, darting upwards nearly perpendicularly, a perfect cloud of feathers coming out of him. He then came wheeling in a stupefied manner over our heads. We both of us fired together at him, and down he fell with one wing broken, and hit all over with our small shot. He struggled hard to keep up with the other wing, but could not do so, and came heavily to the ground within a yard of the edge of the precipice. He fell over on his back at first and then rising to his feet, looked round with an air of reproachful defiance. The blood was dropping slowly out of his beak, when Donald foolishly ran to secure him, instead of leaving him to die where he was; in consequence of his doing so, the eagle fluttered back a few steps, still, however, keeping his face to the foe. But coming to the edge of the precipice, he fell backwards over it, and we saw him tumbling and struggling downwards as he strove to cling to the projections of the rock—but in vain, as he came to no stop until he reached the bottom, where we beheld him, after regaining his feet for a short time, sink gradually to the ground. It was impossible to reach the place where he lay dead without going so far round that the daylight would have failed us. I must own, notwithstanding the reputed destructiveness of the eagle, that I looked with great regret at the dead body of the noble bird, and wished that I had not killed him, the more especially as I was obliged to leave him to rot uselessly in that inaccessible place.'

St John was a remarkable man, as a sportsman-naturalist far ahead of his time, yet on occasions like that one cannot help feeling, had he been alive today, that he would have made an intriguing patient for a psychiatrist.

Charles St John was well aware of the bleak prospects for the ospreys when on his tour of Sutherland in 1849. On leaving Inchnadamph on route to Scourie he describes how he walked ahead of the party:

> 'to look at the osprey's nest on the old castle, and an interesting site it is,

though I lamented the absence of the old birds. Why the poor osprey should be persecuted I know not, as it is quite harmless, living wholly on fish, of which every one knows there is too great an abundance in this country for the most rigid preserver to grudge this picturesque bird its share. The fact probably is that his skin is worth something to keepers and others, as they can always get a few shillings for it, and therefore the bird is doomed to destruction. The "aura sacra fames" will soon put an end to his race in this country.'

Prophetic words, no doubt, but St John himself was not backward in helping them to come true, as we shall see. The eyrie referred to was on the ruins of Ardvreck Castle, about a mile out of Inchnadamph. It had been a traditional nesting site for a long period and was certainly used as late as the 1830s, if not once or twice during the following decade. St John wrote:

> 'On the summit of the highest part of the wall is an immense pile of weather-beaten and bleached sticks, which two years ago formed an osprey's nest, but, unluckily, this most interesting bird has been killed or driven from its exposed nesting place. Nothing could be more characteristic of the bird than this nest, perched on the highest corner of the ruin, overhanging the broad lake, which abounds with trout of all sizes.'

If we accept St John's statement that ospreys used this site in 1847, that was the last time, for sure. Although St John appeared to be ignorant of the fact, by 1849 the osprey in Sutherland was on its last legs. Its only chance of staging any sort of recovery would have required a complete cessation of all the ruthless persecution it was having to take. St John and Dunbar did their best to ensure that should not happen.

After leaving Inchnadamph, the party arrived at Kylesku at midday, where:

> 'having rested our horse and drank *tea* (the only meal we could get) at the ferry-house, we managed to persuade the landlord, who was also the ferryman, to leave the hot whisky and water he was drinking with some acquaintance of his own at that hour, twelve (*sic*) and ferry us across.
>
> We entered into conversation with a shepherd on the north side of the ferry, who told us of a nest of the "Eagle Fisher", as he called it, on an island in a loch not very far from the road; so we appointed the man to meet us the following morning at a certain place . . .'

They spent that night at the inn in Scourie, where the landlord bore the unlikely name of Tough. But Mr Tough kept an excellent house, 'most cleanly and comfortable' and the people were 'full of civility'. What happened on the following morning is told by St John:

> 'At daylight, according to appointment, I started with Mr Dunbar in the boat, but drawn by a small Highland pony whose services we had engaged, for the purpose of getting to the nest of the "Eagle Fisher", as the osprey is sometimes called in Gaelic. At the nearest point of the road to the lake we unshipped the boat, and making traces out of rope, we fastened the pony to it, leaving the undercarriage and wheels by the roadside; we then managed to get the boat to the water's edge, the pony scrambling in a manner practised only by mountain-bred ponies, over bog and rock, dragging the boat after him, while we did our utmost to keep it from injury, or from getting stuck in the rough ground.
>
> 'I was delighted beyond expression at seeing the two ospreys, one of them in the nest and the other soaring above the loch, uttering cries of alarm at our approach.

Soaring through the air, an osprey displays its distinctive marking
(Photograph by Brian Hawkes/The Natural History Photographic Agency)

Loch na Claise Carnaich, looking south-west

'The nest was placed in a most curious situation. About a hundred and fifty yards from the shore there rose from the deep water a solitary rock about ten feet high, shaped like a broken sugar-loaf or truncated one: on the summit of this was the nest—a pile of sticks of very great depth, evidently the accumulation of many breeding seasons, as the osprey returns, year after year, to the same nest. How this heap of sticks withstood the winter gales without being blown at once into the water, puzzled me. In a crevice of the rock was a small tuft or two of green, otherwise it was perfectly bare and steep.

'We launched our little bark, and were soon pulling strongly against a head wind across the loch. The female osprey allowed us to approach within two hundred yards or so, and then leaving her nest, sailed upwards with a circling flight, till she joined her mate high above us.

'Having reached the rock, and with some difficulty ascended to the nest, our disappointment may be imagined when we found it empty. From the old bird having remained on so long, we had made sure of finding eggs on it. The nest itself, however, was interesting to me, perched as it was on the very summit of the rock, and composed of large sticks, every one of which must have been a heavy burden for a bird the size of the osprey. In the centre of the pile of sticks was a cup-shaped hollow, the size of a boy's cap, lined with moss and dead grass, and apparently ready

> to receive eggs. It was of no use lamenting, so we turned our boat towards the landing place, and drifted back quickly in silence. Some hooded crows, perceiving that both the ospreys were off their nest, immediately made a dash towards it, and I was much amused at seeing the skirmishing between these mischievous and cunning marauders and the two ospreys; the latter fighting simply *pro aris et focis*, having no eggs or young to defend; while the crows fought lustily in the hope of finding something in the nest, calculating, probably, as we had done, that the ospreys would not have been sitting on an empty nest.'

There is at least a moral for the modern bird-watcher in this narrative: do not presume, when approaching a nest simply for the gratification of seeing the eggs *in situ* (which was certainly not the apparently innocent intent that St John had in mind) that no harm will come from the exploit. It is evident from St John's chronicles that if almost all birds of prey were rapidly decreasing in numbers in the Highlands during his lifetime, some to the point of extinction, crows seemed to be as common, if not even more numerous, than they are today. It is unfortunate that those people who, understandably, were anxious to increase the stocks of red grouse should have expended so much energy in shooting and trapping birds of prey and destroying their eggs instead of concentrating their attentions on the crows, which were likely to be much more harmful to their interests. No doubt, when the shooters arrived in August, the maggoty corpse of a golden eagle or an osprey rotting away on the vermin-gibbet might look much more impressive and it was also probably easier to shoot or trap an eagle than to kill half a dozen wily crows.

This abortive foray after a clutch of osprey eggs near Scourie took place on May 17. It would seem improbable that any normal hen would not have completed her clutch long before that date. It is just possible, of course, that the particular female was old and barren. However, it seems much more likely that she had already been robbed of her first clutch when they were still fresh, had refurbished the cup of the eyrie and was about to lay a repeat clutch. On the other hand her activities may have had no more significance than in the case of the 'frustration' nests which will be described in the next section of this book.

Both St John and Dunbar (we hear very little about the third member of the party, Mr J., except that he seemed to occupy a good deal of his time fishing, often with considerable success) were both determined men, unlikely to be daunted by a single reverse, nor diverted from their purpose. So it was with the ospreys. Certainly they never wasted their opportunities.

Before leaving Scourie and its 'comfortable hostel' St John relates that:

> 'One of the Duke of Sutherland's foresters brought in a very fine white-tailed (sea) eagle, which he had shot the day before: unluckily the plumage was quite destroyed in consequence of the keeper having, to "make sure", discharged his gun at the bird a second time, after it had fallen, in consequence of which the head was nearly blown off. I procured, however, some feathers for the large salmon fly which we fish with in the Spey river, in making which the eagle's feather is the principal material employed.'

If any person should ever attempt to write a history of the exploitation of uncommon and rare birds in this country they should not ignore the part played by some fishermen. It is true that anglers mostly only contributed indirectly to this unsavoury business by helping to provide a market but they can hardly be regarded as blameless. Anyway, here was one sea-eagle that was not destined to gather dust in Mr Hancock's famous museum.

The party left Scourie early on the morning of May 18 with the intention of reaching Durness that evening. They reckoned they could not afford the time to visit the island of Handa and its huge colonies of 'sea-fowl' but the landlord of the inn at Scourie had told them of another osprey nest on an island in a loch which was only a mile off their road. The bait was too tempting to miss, so they left their boat in charge of a 'bare-legged and bare-headed boy' at a small bridge some three miles north-east of Scourie, proceeding on foot to spy out the land, finding a vantage point overlooking the loch:

> 'We immediately through a glass discovered the nest of the osprey, built in exactly a similar situation to the last; that is, on the summit of a rock about eight feet high, shaped like a truncated cone, and standing exposed and alone in the loch. On coming nearer, we could distinguish the white head of the female osprey on the nest. The male bird was not in view. I was determined that I should remain concealed near the loch, while my two companions went for the boat. This plan was adopted for the double reason that I might be at hand to shoot any hooded crow who might attempt to take the eggs whilst the osprey was off, she having left the nest on our approach, and also that I might have a chance of shooting the old osprey herself in case she came within shot. I must say that I would rather she had escaped this fate; but as her skin was wanted, I agreed to try to kill her.
>
> 'For some time after the departure of my companions she flew round and round at a great height, occasionally drifting away with the high wind

and then returning to the loch. She passed two or three times, not very far from me, before I shot at her. But at last I fired, and the poor bird, after wheeling blindly about for a few moments, fell far to leeward of me, and down amongst the most precipitous and rocky part of the mountain, quite dead. She was scarcely down behind the cliffs when I heard the cry of an

Preparing to take aim at an osprey's nest—the bad old days!

osprey in quite a different direction, and on looking that way I saw the male bird flying up from a great distance. As he came nearer I could distinguish with my glass that he was carrying a fish in his claws. On approaching he redoubled his cries, probably expecting the well-known answer, or signal of gratitude, from his mate; but not hearing her, he flew on till he came immediately over the nest. I could plainly see him turning his head to the right and left, as if looking for her, and as if in astonishment at her unwonted absence. He came lower and lower, still holding the fish in his feet, which were stretched out at full length from his body. Not seeing her, he again ascended and flew to the other end of the lake, then flew away far out of sight, still keeping possession of the fish. He probably went to look for the female at some known and frequented haunt, as he flew rapidly off, in a direct line. He soon, however, came over the lake again, and continued his flight to and fro and his loud cries for above an hour, still keeping the fish ready for his mate. I at length heard the voices of my friends, and we soon launched the boat. The osprey became much agitated as we neared the rock where the nest was, and dropped the fish he held into the water. We found two beautiful eggs in the nest, of a roundish shape; the colour white, with numerous spots and marks of a fine rich red brown. As we came away we still observed the male bird unceasingly calling and seeking for his hen. I was really sorry I had shot her.'

This account of a spirited but ruthless adventure is made more sickening because the corpse of the female was never recovered. Taking the eggs from the nest was bad enough but the futile shooting of the hen was an even greater setback to the prospect of ospreys retaining their toe-hold in Sutherland. This was 1848 and the species really was doomed, because there is no evidence of a pair attempting to breed in the county—a stronghold for the osprey less than a hundred years earlier—after 1850. If St John and Dunbar were not the only ones who were exterminating the Scottish osprey, they were certainly taking on more than their fair share of the job.

They went through Rhiconich to Durness, having spotted an osprey fishing in the Laxford river; they did not stop, so that one must conclude that the bird was far out of shot. From Durness their track skirted the eastern shore of Loch Hope and on to Loch Maddie (or Meadie) where they found some more greylag geese nesting. They also discovered the gravestone of another pair of ospreys:

> 'In one island, containing a few stunted birch trees, we saw an old osprey's nest, not now tenanted; but I am told that the old birds were inhabiting it two years ago. The nest was most interesting: it was placed in the fork of a tree so low that we could see into it without climbing, and it consisted of a perfect cart-load of sticks, varying from the size of a very stout walking-stick down to the twigs of birch and heather of which the inner part of the fabric was composed. I did not measure the nest, but as nearly as I could guess, it was not less than eight feet in length, and nearly four in width; the depth too was very great; the inner lining was

Shooting a hapless osprey beside a loch near Rhiconich

composed of a coarse kind of grass that grows in these islands. Although the nest must have weathered many a winter storm of wind, snow, and rain, and was quite bleached, it was still fixed firmly in the branch of a birch tree. To have seen the ospreys building up this great and strong mass would have repaid one for a journey of many a long mile.'

Charles St John was an intelligent person. Only a few hours before he came across the remarkable but deserted eyrie he had not only taken her clutch of eggs, but had shot a female osprey in a pretty wanton manner. But for the persecution executed by him and his like this nest would probably have been tenanted. His endless lamentations, such as 'I was really sorry I had shot her,' do not ring true.

St John, however, had not yet done harrying the Sutherlandshire ospreys. Unexpectedly, towards the end of May, he had to leave his companions to travel down to the south of England. He returned towards the end of the first week in June:

> 'Travelling (that is, the mere act of passing along the road) takes up very little of your time nowadays. You go from London to Edinburgh in about thirteen hours, and a good steamer takes the traveller from Granton Pier to Invergordon in Ross-shire quickly and comfortably enough; that is, I left Granton at 6.0 a.m. on the 16th, and landed in Invergordon early in the evening of the 7th . . .'

On June 9 he rejoined his two companions, Dunbar and Mr J., at the inn at Lairg. They then more or less retraced their tracks back to Scourie. This time they contrived to take a look at the sea birds on Handa Island but St John remembered the loch a few miles from Scourie where he had recently shot the female osprey and taken her two eggs. If he really regretted murdering that hen, one can only guess what might have prompted him to return to the scene of this ugly exploit:

> 'Two miles from Scourie, on the Rhiconnich road or near it, is a loch where the ospreys build, and where, in May, I shot the old hen, taking at the same time two eggs. Mr Dunbar, with his usual perseverance, went to this nest immediately on our return from Handa and found that the male had got another mate, and that she was already busily employed in sitting on a single egg.
>
> 'It is very difficult to describe correctly the eggs of many birds: for instance, the two eggs which I took from this nest were beautifully marked with fine rich red spots, while the egg now taken by Dunbar was of a dirty white colour, marked at one end only by a splash of brown . . .'

This single egg was taken in mid-June, when there could not be the remotest chance of the hen laying another clutch and rearing any young. That there was only one egg suggests either that this female was a very young or a very old bird, or, perhaps, somebody else had not only robbed her of her first clutch but had also shot *her* mate. It is even just possible that this single egg was fresh laid and her clutch was not complete. Possibly inspired by the taking of his second osprey clutch of the tour, they went off to examine a nest near the Kylesku ferry which they had observed in May:

> 'On looking at it with a glass, we saw one old bird sitting, *not standing*, on the nest and yet on Dunbar's swimming out to it he found no egg in the nest, which was exactly in the same state as when we left it three or four weeks ago; both birds, too, continued sailing and screaming over our heads, as if they had eggs or young ones to defend. This nest, like the last three that we had seen, was built on the same kind of conical rock, standing out of the waters of the lake . . .'

Had this nest, in fact, contained a clutch of eggs we can surmise that Dunbar would have doffed his cap, folded it carefully round the eggs and swum back to shore with the cap held between his teeth. That these two ospreys had hung around the eyrie for at least five weeks strongly suggests that the hen was robbed of her clutch almost as soon as they were laid and before St John and his companions had first come across them. In the long interval between their two visits the female possibly laid a repeat set and these, too, had been plundered. Did it really matter? Ospreys had become so rare that collectors or shepherds and other persons who eked out their meagre pittances by dealing in the eggs, were almost queueing up to get the last of the golden eggs.

St John was such a curious mixture of the good and the bad that it would be hard to pass a fair judgement on his exploits. He was a good sportsman—and not a greedy one either. He is certainly one of the great field naturalists of the nineteenth century and he could write well. His books are not only readable but very valuable. It might be only fair to let Charles St John have the last word:

> 'It is difficult to determine how far we are right in endeavouring utterly to destroy one kind of animal or bird in order to increase another species. Nature, if left to herself, keeps up a fair equilibrium and proportion amongst all her productions; and, without doubt, if the world were left to itself without the interference of mankind, there would never be an undue proportion of any one kind of living creature: the birds of prey would keep down the granivorous birds from increasing till they devoured all the fruits of the earth; and the carnivorous birds and beasts would never entirely extirpate any other species, as their own numbers would be lessened by want of food before this could happen; besides which, we see that unless artificial measures are resorted to, the number of living animals always bears proportion to, and is regulated by, the supply of food which offers itself and, as these supplies fail, there is a natural tendency for the consumers to cease increasing, or betake themselves to other regions. But when man comes in as an active agent, he gradually extirpates all beasts and birds of

prey for the purpose of protecting and causing to increase the weaker but more useful animals and birds. In this country, for instance, we can no more afford to allow hawks and crows, foxes and weasels to flourish, however picturesque and beautiful they may be, than we could afford to allow poppies or other useless but ornamental wild flowers to overrun our cornfields . . .

'I cannot say that I am at all anxious to see our island entirely clear of what all game-preservers call "vermin". There is more beauty and more to interest one in the flight and habits of a pair of falcons than in a whole pack of grouse; and I regret constantly to see how rare these birds, and eagles, and many others, are daily becoming, under the influence of traps, poison and guns. The edict which has gone forth against them is far too comprehensive and sweeping, and many perfectly innocent birds go to swell the gamekeeper's list of "vermin".'

This is fair, level-headed stuff, all the more remarkable bearing in mind that it was written 140 years ago, a long time before the science of ecology first spluttered into existence. Unfortunately there were too many occasions when St John appeared to be incapable of leaving Nature to itself and all too often, when it came down to the extirpation of species, he was certainly a very active agent. Man is born to sin; it might be as well if we left it at that.

Osgood Mackenzie, born in 1842, third son of Sir Francis Mackenzie, laird of Gairloch in Wester Ross, was another persecutor of rare birds although he lacked some of the dogged persistence of St John. Osgood was the instigator of the famous semi-tropical gardens at Inverewe—a legacy to posterity for which many sins may be forgiven.

Mackenzie's book, *A Hundred Years in the Highlands*, was first published in 1921 and has been reprinted many times. It makes excellent reading in its own right but we are only here concerned with one or two pertinent references to birds of prey and the backcloth against which their persecution took place. Osgood records:

'Birds'-nesting expeditions were also made to the islands of Loch Maree after ospreys' eggs. There were two eyries there, one of them in a real curiosity of a place—namely, in Eilean Suthainn, one of the biggest of the islands in Loch Maree. There is a small loch, and in this loch (the depth of which is about double that of the neighbouring Loch Maree), there is an island on which stood one big Scots fir. In it was the osprey's nest, as large as a waggon-wheel, with three eggs. It was lined with lumps of wool

> and bits of cow-dung, and lying at the foot of the tree I found a dead mallard, which appeared to have been freshly killed by the ospreys. There was another fir-tree where they bred on a promontory nearly opposite Loch Maree, from which I got two eggs. But alas! the birds have been extinct in that region for at least sixty-four years.'

That word 'Alas!' may be a slightly indigestible hiccough, but Mackenzie's report makes it clear that ospreys had ceased to breed in the Loch Maree neighbourhood by the 1850s.

Osgood Mackenzie entered on life almost too late to exploit ospreys—but not quite:

> 'When I was not more than seven or eight years old, I was already quite a keen collector of eggs, and greatly coveted a clutch of those of the sea-eagle, which were always rare in this district, whereas the golden eagles were comparatively plentiful. I have known only one other nesting-place of the sea-eagles on this coast, where in a sea-cliff they continued to breed till within comparatively modern times. I gave my dear mother no peace until she had arranged an expedition to the nest; it was just beyond our march, but permission having been got from our neighbour, away we went on pony-back, with an expert rock-climber and ropes, etc. Though the precipice from the pinnacle of Spidean Moirich down to Loch an Doire (Lake of the Withered Grove) at its base cannot be much under two thousand feet of nearly plumb rock, the eagles had fortunately chosen for their eyrie a fairly accessible shelf near the bottom. But, on our arrival we found we were just a day too late, for a south country shepherd from the other property, having got wind that eagles' eggs had a certain market value, had taken them the previous day. However, a good Caledonian bank-note, if it had *Tir nam beann, nan gleann s'nan qaisqach* (the land of the mountains, the glens, and the heroes) printed on it, was fairly powerful in those days; and for a pound-note of that description my enemy, Jock Beattie (for I fear I hated him in my little heart), handed over the two big, pure white eggs, and I returned home in a kind of semi-triumph on my Shetland pony's back. Just below the north end of the Fionn Loch, which is but one of the many lochs in that wild stretch of moorland, is Loch an Iasgair (the Osprey's Loch). In Gaelic the osprey is called Ailein Iasgair (Allen the Fisherman). How well I remember the excitement over the arrival at Poolewe Inn of Lord Huntingfield and a Mr Corrance—both, I think, from Suffolk—the first egg-collectors who ever came to this country.

Hearing of the ospreys, they made at once for the loch, where the nest was built on a high stack of rock rising sheer out of the water. Their valet swam out, and returned with the two eggs safely in his cap, which he held between his teeth.'

Loch an Iasgair, near Gairloch

At the beginning of the nineteenth century ospreys were breeding—in some cases in small numbers, maybe, but certainly regularly—in seven counties: Dunbarton, Kirkcudbright, Perthshire, Inverness-shire, Argyll, Ross and Cromarty, and Sutherland. They were probably still nesting or attempting to nest in Stirlingshire and Kinross, possibly in three or four other counties, including Moray and Elgin but one cannot be sure on the meagre evidence available. Some of that evidence, too, is conflicting.

Sir William Jardine, in 1841, wrote: 'crossing the Forth we shall find a pair at least frequenting each of the larger lochs; and in Ross-shire and Sutherland, they are even more abundant. In some districts, four or five may be seen in the course of a day.' Hasty and uncritical consumption of such airy-fairy nonsense might give the impression that, even as late as the early 1840s, the osprey was still flourishing north of Edinburgh. There is the implication not only that every large loch held at least a breeding pair but that some held two pairs, which is even more improbable. If ospreys were even more abundant in Ross and Cromarty and Sutherland (again unlikely) it is puzzling to guess at what could have happened to them all in the eight years that elapsed prior to St John's famous tour. Jardine was almost certainly writing 'guide-book' copy from the comfort of an armchair and it would be a mistake to take his remarks too seriously. Look what was happening elsewhere.

Ospreys had ceased to breed at Loch Lomond early in the century and had almost certainly been driven out of Dunbartonshire around 1810. In Argyllshire, if we accept the evidence of Selby, certainly one of our few reliable witnesses, two pairs were still breeding in the early 1830s, one eyrie being in the Pass of Brander and the other on the ruins of Kilchurn castle, both sites adjacent to Loch Awe. Selby says these nests were often robbed, a statement which there is no need to dispute, so it is not surprising that neither survived for long. Tenuous evidence might suggest that a pair of ospreys tried to breed at Loch Awe in 1850 and it matters little as to whether or not we accept that record. Effectively the species had been driven out of Argyll some years before St John and Dunbar went on the rampage in Sutherland. In Kirkcudbrightshire the evidence is even more sketchy, although the odd pair or two might still have been trying to breed in the 1840s. In the *New Statistical Account* of 1841 the osprey was said to breed on the islets in Loch Grannoch, between Newton Stewart and New Galloway, and in Loch Skerrow. There are no strong grounds to doubt that both of these were traditional sites for ospreys and for a long while they must have represented the southern limit to the breeding-range of ospreys in Britain, yet the *Statistical Account* cannot be relied on as sound evidence that they were still nesting there as late as 1840. However, it seems possible that ospreys may have nested in the Loch Enoch area, on the borders of Ayrshire, much later than that. Gray and Anderson, in their *Birds of Ayrshire and Wigtownshire*, published in 1869, stated that in 1854 an osprey was still frequenting Loch Doon in Ayrshire, which was an easy osprey flight from Loch Enoch:

> 'one bird at least might have been seen fishing in the loch—thought to be the male in quest of prey to carry to his mate incubating on an islet in a small loch in Kirkcudbright where we have good reason for saying a frequented eyrie still exists.'

The good reasons are not given; lacking them, one really must presume it improbable that birds were attempting to nest in the county as late as 1869. It seems much more likely that nesting in the county ceased in the 1840s, if not earlier.

In Perthshire ospreys must surely have bred in some strength in former times, although even to hint at the possible number of birds breeding, in a large and generally suitable county as regards habitat, would be little better than guesswork. Any reliable indication as to when the species ceased to breed in Perthshire is even harder to come by than in most other areas but the Lake of Menteith, a few miles east of Aberfoyle, was certainly a traditional site to which birds may have returned even as late as the 1840s.

In Ross and Cromarty there were a number of well-known breeding sites: Loch Maree to the east of Gairloch; Glen Shiel; Loch an Iasgair and Loch Luichart, to the north of Strathcarron. The picturesque railway line running from Inverness to the Kyle of Lochalsh runs alongside the northern shores of Luichart, which was the only site for breeding ospreys in Ross and Cromarty after the 1840s. Harvie-Brown, who is unfortunately somewhat unreliable, alleged that two ospreys were shot at Luichart in 1865. Whether regular breeding or attempted breeding continued every year is a matter for doubt, but George Waterston accepted that ospreys last bred here as late as 1892 and a single bird returned in both the two following years.

In Sutherland the ospreys were finished by 1850 at the latest. One of the last traditional sites in the county to be used was that on the ruins of Ardvreck Castle, near Inchnadamph. John Wolley was there in 1849 and actually saw an osprey but it showed no interest in the old nest. The following year Wolley was told that the last time this site had been used by a pair of ospreys was in 1848, but even this is open to doubt, as hearsay evidence often is. In the third week of May of that year, as I have already written, St John and Dunbar visited Ardvreck and saw no birds. However, they were there again in the middle of June and St John records that 'I was much pleased at seeing one osprey on the nest and another sailing over the loch'. If this female laid eggs it seems unlikely that she was successful in hatching them. The dramatic collapse of nesting ospreys in Sutherland in the late 1840s is a measure of the persecution to which they were subjected.

Excluding Loch Luichart, for which remarkably little information is available—which really is surprising if ospreys were at least attempting to nest in most years, for this loch has always been both well known and reasonably accessible—excluding Luichart the history of the ospreys in Scotland after 1850 is, within our knowledge, almost wholly confined to Inverness-shire, where ospreys hung on with surprising tenacity for many, many years at three

A pair of ospreys on their eyrie
(Photograph by Eric Hosking)

sites: Loch an Eilean, Loch Arkaig and Loch Loyne. Fortunately the lairds concerned were genuinely interested in these birds and concerned about their welfare, taking what steps they could to safeguard them. Ospreys had by now become the rarest breeding species in all Britain. This added greatly to the value of the swag and the competition to acquire what so easily might have been the last clutch of osprey eggs ever to be laid in Britain was certainly keen enough. It would be unfair to the oologists to declare that all collecting of eggs was unscientific, but much of it was. In the case of rare species it was conducted solely for personal gratification or financial gain. That much is clear from the fairly well documented history of the Speyside ospreys during the latter half of the last century. In compiling the following summary I acknowledge my indebtedness to George Waterston.

Lewis Dunbar, brother of St John's faithful companion William, robbed the ospreys at the eyrie on the ruined castle on the islet in Loch an Eilean in five consecutive seasons, 1848–52. Dunbar, for all that is known to the contrary, might have repeated his performance in the summer of 1853, but he left for Australia towards the end of that year. His departure cannot have done the birds any harm, but the heat was on with a vengeance, so that what might otherwise have been providential may have made little or no difference in the long run.

In 1848 Dunbar, who, like his brother, was obviously resourceful and a man of courage and great fortitude, took at least two clutches in Speyside where, in addition to the birds at the Loch an Eilean eyrie, another pair had built an eyrie in the ruined lodge adjacent to Loch Morlich. Having taken this clutch, Dunbar turned his attention to the other pair, walking twenty miles from Grantown-on-Spey to Loch an Eilean. According to Harvie-Brown, Dunbar told him how he swam out through what must have been icy cold water, got his bare legs badly stung by nettles crawling about among the ruins whilst making up his mind about the best way to reach the nest, climbed up, took the eggs, put them in his bonnet which he then placed on his head and swam back to the shore. All this was accomplished in broad daylight.

The following year, 1849, two pairs were again nesting. The Morlich pair deserted their traditional site on the lodge, building their eyrie in an old pine close by the loch. Dunbar had this lot first and apparently sent them off to Charles St John and they finished up in Mr Hancock's museum at Newcastle. Then he robbed the Loch an Eilean birds on May 24.

In 1850 Dunbar continued to provide more coal for Newcastle. For the third year running he took the Loch an Eilean clutch, these three eggs going to Mr Hancock. There is no evidence that the Glenmore eyries were used that year but John Hancock himself came up to join Dunbar in a bit more pillaging designed to add to his growing and famous (some might say infamous) collection. In his *Reminiscences* Dunbar wrote:

> 'Mr Hancock met me and we started on a nesting tour through Abernethy, and landed at Ryvoan, the nearest house to Cairngorm, which we made our base of operations. We visited an old dam at the head of the river Nethy. On the edge of the dam we found two old ospreys' nests on two very stunted and blasted fir trees. Mr Hancock took a sketch of both trees and nests. Next day we made for Loch Morlich, where the osprey built on the chimney of an old, burnt-down shooting lodge, situated at the

> east end of the loch. I climbed up and found only two eggs in the nest, so I left them. Mr Hancock was very anxious to get the old bird, so I was put in ambush while the two accompanying me walked away about half a mile. I had not long to wait; and as the hen was coming down to the nest I shot her with a walking-stick gun which I invariably carried, left her on the ground, and secured the two eggs. By this time, Mr Hancock came up and took a sketch of the bird as she lay dead on the ground, and with a broken wing. On dissecting this bird when he got home, he found another egg, beautifully marked and quite ready for laying.'

The following year, 1851, there were again two pairs in the Rothiemurchus area but, once more due to the Dunbar brothers, neither was successful. William sent John Wolley a single egg which had been taken by a shepherd from an eyrie near Loch Morlich, leaving the redoubtable Lewis Dunbar to rob the Loch an Eilean pair, the two eggs being sent to John Wolley. Alfred Newton gives Wolley's account of this in Part I of *Ootheca Wolleyana* (1864):

> 'These two beautiful eggs I obtained from a correspondent (Lewis Dunbar) on 3 May, 1851, they being the only result of a ten days' nesting expedition undertaken by him. *He took them at three o'clock in the morning* of 29th April 1851, at the ruins of an old castle on an island in an Inverness-shire loch. *After walking nearly all night* he reached the spot in the middle of a snowstorm; and having tied a cord to his life-preserver, he swam off, leaving the other end in charge of a man on the shore. On the island, he tied the rope to a stone and climbed up the ruins, *slipping about in six inches of snow*. Having found two eggs in the nest, he discovered that he had left his cap behind him. He tried one egg in his mouth but could not breathe with it; and at last he swam ashore on his back with an egg in each hand. He blew the eggs in the boathouse, washing out the inside with whisky. *He had taken these eggs for four years, and the old birds have always had a second brood.* The first or second year, an old woman saw him come out of the water, and ran into the cottage; since then he has always gone earlier in the morning, and no-one has known anything about it. He was exceedingly anxious that I should go early one morning and see him take the other egg or eggs out of the nest for me; but considering my position there, I declined —the more so as I suspected the proprietress protected the birds; and I have been since assured that there was a man appointed on purpose to take care of them . . .'

A male osprey using his strong talons to scratch himself
(Photograph by C. K. Mylne)

It is useful to interrupt Wolley's account for a moment to discuss one or two points. The behaviour of Dunbar in robbing these nests of their eggs is not as disreputable as it might seem. Apart from the courage and daring of some of his exploits, he was probably in need of the money. It was people like Wolley and St John, who paid these men to do the dirty work for them, who must take the blame—and well they deserve it. Most of them were educated persons, capable of appreciating the dire consequences of these incessant raids on the eggs of ospreys and other rare birds. Wolley was far worse than St John because he was a voracious collector in his own right; if his conscience allowed him to cloak his actions under the excuse that his motives were scientific, one can only say that that particular cloak was uncommonly thin.

Wolley seized on Dunbar's statement that, after taking a clutch for four consecutive years, the birds had always laid again. Almost since the beginning—or so, at least, it seems—this has been a favourite trumpet-call of most oologists. Perhaps it salves uneasy consciences or else is intended to mollify public opinion. Many birds, more especially those with relatively short incubation and fledging periods, will lay a repeat clutch, although that clutch may well not be as large as the first one and the chances of success may be proportionately lower. Few collectors, finding the nest of a rare species containing eggs rather late in the season would be likely to stay their itching hands on the grounds that it might be a second clutch, the first having already been taken by another member of their own fraternity. There is, furthermore, considerable doubt whether a female osprey would lay a second clutch unless her first had been robbed when very fresh. This is not to suggest that ospreys never 'repeat'. Second clutches are usually smaller and the odds on rearing young successfully are almost certainly less, as the later a brood of ospreys are airborne the lower may be their chances of ultimate survival.

Lewis Dunbar said that the ospreys he robbed always laid again. In 1849 he plundered eggs on May 24. If this female laid another clutch she would have been unlikely to have completed it much before the end of the first week in June and her prospects of rearing a brood of young would have been remote. Reluctantly, one is bound to suspect the veracity of Dunbar on this particular point; he had probably been 'brain-washed' by some of his customers.

We may pick up John Wolley's account, following his receipt of the two osprey eggs taken by Dunbar at Loch an Eilean on May 3, 1851:

> 'After I had finally refused his offer (Dunbar's suggestion that he should accompany him on one of his forays), he mentioned incidentally that Mr R. Gordon-Cumming had got into a great scrape for harrying this nest some years before. The day after I got the eggs, Mr Edge and I went to the loch; we got to the side of it most distant from the castle, but we saw the head of the osprey on the nest looking about in every direction. The cottage was just beyond the castle from where we were. We then came back round the loch; and as we got near, the bird rose and left the nest, which was now very conspicuous; but she soon lighted on it again and settled herself down. The wind was bitterly cold and it was constantly snowing and hailing. I made a sketch of the place; whilst I was doing so the cock bird came up and alighted on an adjoining part of the wall, first putting down his long claws. The distance of the castle from the shore might be one hundred and twenty yards; the old doorway was on a level with the water; but the whole loch was then somewhat dammed up by a kind of weir. At one time both birds were flying at once. We went to the house and saw the old woman before mentioned, who told us that one morning, several years before, she saw "a chiel" coming out of the water, who had been to the nest.'

These Loch an Eilean ospreys were so ruthlessly harried that it is astonishing they continued to survive. However, although they must have been robbed of almost every clutch of eggs one gets the impression that, unlike the last survivors in Sutherland (and probably elsewhere) they largely escaped the attentions of those who, armed with shotguns, were after the skins of adults or young either for museum collections or for their own personal gratification. Anyway, after four successive summers of highly successful harassment, the pair returned again in 1852. This was the last time that Lewis Dunbar robbed this, the most famous of all the old Highland osprey sites, and his own account of the exploit can be found in Newton's *Ootheca Wolleyana*:

> 'The three eggs I took myself on the night of 8th May 1852, between eleven and twelve o'clock. As it was very dark and no moon, I had the precaution to take my cousin along with me, and he proved a great service. I took off my clothes and put on my life-preserver, attaching a cord to the back of it. By the help of a fusee I was able to distinguish that the time I was about to launch my carcase into the water was twenty-five minutes to twelve. I got over quite safe. The cock bird flew away before I reached the island; and after I had climbed up to the top of the ruin, and was just at the nest, I put my hand out to catch the hen, but when she felt me she gave a loud scream and flew away also. On arriving at the island I had fixed the cord to a bush; and on coming back I had some difficulty in finding it owing to the darkness of the night, but when I did so, I secured it to my belt and bawled to my cousin to pull, which he did. In the middle I was taken with cramp, but he succeeded in hauling me out. After dressing, we forded the river, which was very high at the time, and on going across with my cousin on my back, I stumbled, and down he went, but he managed to get to his feet; and this put an end to our adventure.'

Insofar as the lamentable story of the Scottish ospreys is concerned, Lewis Dunbar now leaves the stage; for all his apparent villainy, he earns a round of applause. He was, all said and done, a tremendous character. Physically, he must have been immensely strong and it is impossible not to admire both his courage and tenacity of purpose. From his own account of this final raid it would appear that, in pitch darkness, he made an attempt to take the female as she sat—astonishingly tightly in view of what was going on—brooding her three eggs. The osprey is a large and powerful bird with formidable talons and one might presume that few men, given the opportunity, would have the nerve even to contemplate such an undertaking—in pitch darkness, too!

By now the future of the Scottish ospreys was critical. Wolley died in 1859 and throughout the previous six years, according to Newton, none of his many Scottish correspondents ever mentioned ospreys during that long period. Newton even says that Wolley was under the impression that ospreys had become extinct as a breeding species in Britain but it seems at least more probable that the odd pair or two maintained a precarious toe-hold. The fact that there is no record of any nesting at Loch an Eilean from 1853 until 1862 cannot be accepted as evidence that the site was tenantless. On the contrary, it would seem likely that once the sequence was completely broken the site would probably be abandoned. However, the maintenance of the sequence would not require either that the birds should nest every year or even that a pair must be present. Ospreys must have been at some risk of being shot or trapped outside the breeding season, as well as facing other hazards. Anyway, a pair who lost their eggs year after year would be growing older. If a cock returned to the eyrie, the hen might have perished in some way or other and, bearing in mind the decimation that was going on, he might fail to secure a mate, possibly for several years in succession. Yet the site-sequence would still be maintained due to the cock bird's attachment to the eyrie. There are plenty of examples, both in the past and more recent history of British ospreys to suggest that, as a rule, the cock is the first to return to the eyrie where he awaits the arrival of the female. If, probably because a disaster has overtaken her, the female does not put in an appearance after a reasonable interval, evidence suggests that the cock goes hunting, probably over a wide area, in search of a new mate. By the middle of the nineteenth century, if not before, it must have become increasingly difficult for a male that had lost his partner to find a new one. At that time very few young birds left the nest, let alone survived to maturity.

Records of the Speyside ospreys are somewhat thinly documented throughout the last half of the nineteenth century. Loch an Eilean birds not only nested in 1863 but probably reared at least one chick. There is then nothing of note until 1879, when this pair may have bred successfully because the birds were present from April until September. The birds nested again the following year and reared two young. They returned in 1881, although the results are not known. In 1885 or 1886 ospreys may have nested at Loch Gamnha, just above Loch an Eilean. It might seem improbable that two pairs of ospreys would nest so closely, and this Gamnha eyrie could have been built by the Loch an Eilean pair. If so, we can only guess at what might have caused them to desert the traditional eyrie; one cannot exclude the possibility that the new site might have been no more than a 'frustration' eyrie, built after the female had lost her first clutch and did not lay again.

Although it was undoubtedly the most important, most often used and best known eyrie in Speyside, it would be an error to suppose that the Loch an Eilean site (with which I am inclined to bracket Loch Gamnha) was the

An osprey chick on an eyrie
(Photograph by Roger Tory Peterson/Bruce Coleman Limited)

only site in the neighbourhood which was still in use as late as the final decades of the century. In 1885 the then minister of Abernethy, one Rev. Dr Forsyth, informed Harvie-Brown that the birds had bred recently in Abernethy Forest, whilst as late as 1893 Harvie-Brown reported visiting an old eyrie in the thick pines of Rothiemurchus. As the Loch an Eilean pair almost certainly reared young in 1879 and 1880 and might well have done so in 1881—a phenomenal run of successes for any remaining ospreys in those lean times—one might reasonably presume that there were some young, but mature, ospreys in the neighbourhood around the mid-eighties. It is ironical that, had the ospreys been left alone at that time, there may well have been sufficient stock not only for the birds to establish themselves in some strength in mid-Speyside but, in due time, to have spread out into many of their old haunts. It was not to be.

The Loch an Eilean pair laid eggs but were robbed in 1887. In 1888 there were as many as four birds at this site. According to Harvie-Brown's rather colourful and somewhat unsatisfactory account, there was much fighting between the birds and certainly one was attacked fiercely by another and held under the water until it drowned. This happened very early in the year, on

April 7, but if one believes Harvie-Brown's version *both* the birds involved were females. (The dead bird was recovered and stuffed and is still in existence.) According to Harvie-Brown:

> 'In the evening of the same day, a male bird arrived, supposed to be the mate of the conquering hero; and next day a second male, supposed to be the mate of the dead bird, arrived on the scene. The two males fought furiously also, but the end of the contest was not observed.'

Apart from the fact that conquering heroes are usually males there may be rather too much supposition in his story for the critical reader. We might just as well suppose that of the two birds involved in the fight, the survivor was a male already in possession of his territory. We might also speculate that the third bird to arrive on the scene, in the evening after the fight, was a female and that when another male arrived the following day she joined with the conquering hero in driving him off. Supposition, of course, but it fits in rather better with the general pattern of osprey behaviour than Harvie-Brown's version.

It was not until 1894 that there is evidence to indicate that the Loch an Eilean ospreys again bred successfully, bringing off two young. The following summer the pair certainly hatched eggs, whilst in 1896 they successfully reared two young. This was followed by the pair again hatching two young in the following year although it is not known whether they managed to bring the chicks to the free-flying stage. However, the four summers 1894–7 were as good, if not better, than any similar period since the 1840s or earlier. In three of these seasons six chicks had been reared; in the other summer it is only known that chicks hatched out but the laird had always been sympathetic in his attitude to the ospreys, safeguarding the Loch an Eilean eyrie to the best of his admittedly limited ability. Eggs, however, must have been much more vulnerable than young birds, so that one can presume that this pair, in those four halcyon summers, probably reared more than six—perhaps as many as seven or eight. At that time it must have seemed that these hard-pressed Speyside ospreys were about to stage a spirited come-back. The end, in fact, was very close and the birds had nested successfully on the old castle for the last time. Yet if we accept the record as it stands at the end of 1897, it is difficult to offer any plausible explanation for what followed.

Stretching a wing while maintaining a sharp look-out
(Photograph by C. K. Mylne)

In 1897 it has been stated that both birds arrived back at the eyrie on March 29. Apart from the fact that this is an exceptionally early date, it is unusual for both birds of a pair to arrive on the same day and it might be reckoned to be more exceptional so early in the year. By a strange coincidence in 1898 both birds apparently appeared together at the eyrie on exactly the same date. Certainly they must have arrived early because they were watched by two reliable observers on April 9 and during the following three days. Later in the summer, however, the birds were seen to be without young, strongly suggesting that an egg-collector had passed that way. One cannot exclude the possibility, however remote, that the female never laid any eggs at all, which might help to explain why the pair were apparently still together and still attached to the empty eyrie even in high summer. Thus it is possible that the female might have been an old and barren bird. Again, it could be that the cock's mate had perished during the winter and that the female was slightly immature, not yet capable of mating effectively. In-breeding among birds is not uncommon. There must surely have been some young birds around, reared in this very eyrie, even if some of them were immature. Indeed there is a report of four ospreys seen flying together in Glenfeshie, not far to the westward of Loch an Eilean, in that summer of 1898.

Two birds were back at the eyrie in 1899. There was apparently much fighting between the resident pair and a third bird and this is said to have led to the eggs being smashed, which strikes me as a not impossible but rather unlikely tale. Two birds again visited the castle eyrie in 1900 but they did not breed. In both 1901 and 1902 a single osprey returned to the Loch an Eilean eyrie before, with astonishing abruptness, the curtain finally fell on the long drama that had been played out at what was assuredly the most romantic, best known and most historic among all the traditional nesting sites, past or present, which have been used by ospreys in Britain.

The spring of 1900 was the last in which a pair of birds returned to Loch an Eilean. In that year it is probable that ospreys were still trying to breed at three other sites in Inverness-shire. The best known of these was at Loch Arkaig, where the eyrie was afforded some protection by Cameron of Lochiel. Here a pair turned up each year until 1908, after which a single bird, presumably the cock although one cannot be sure that it was the same bird, returned annually to the eyrie until 1913. As already mentioned, ospreys probably returned to Loch Loyne even as late as the First World War, although there is no evidence that might suggest that their efforts met with much success, if any, during the last ten years or so of their tenure. It is likely that

A cock osprey balancing on a branch
(Photograph by Nigel Charles)

ospreys returned to Glencannich for a year or two after the turn of the century.

Immediately following the remarkable run of three or four successful years for the Loch an Eilean birds (1894–7) the Loch Arkaig pair also staged a kind of death-bed rally. In an article published in the magazine, *British Birds,* in 1943, Cameron of Lochiel wrote:

> 'One year there were two pairs: I think that would be about 1899 or 1900. The second pair nested on a tree at the foot of Glen Camagarry about four miles east from the head of the loch. The eggs were stolen from this second nest, as my father sent a boy up the tree to look into the nest and all he found was a stone shaped like an egg. That year there were no fewer than seven ospreys flying about the loch, the two pairs already referred to, two young birds, and an old single solitary bird.'

Throughout the latter half of the nineteenth century it would seem probable that the future of the Scottish ospreys depended almost wholly on our native stock. As they have always done, some of the birds that bred or attempted to breed in Scandinavia must have passed through parts of Britain, perhaps mainly on the eastern seaboard, both on their northward passage in early spring and again on their return in the autumn. However, the Scandinavian ospreys were also subject to much wanton persecution throughout this period, with the inevitable result that numbers were decreasing in Norway and Sweden, albeit more slowly than in Scotland. It seems highly improbable that there was ever any surplus stock in Scandinavia that might have encouraged a few birds to halt and nest in Scotland, where there was plenty of room for them. All this, of course, is speculative but the sudden collapse of the Scottish ospreys around the turn of the century has some puzzling aspects, even if at that time egg-collecting was still as big a threat to their survival as it had ever been. Around 1900 there were the seven free-flying birds seen at Loch Arkaig towards the end of the summer; the Loch an Eilean pair still survived and only a few years earlier had enjoyed unusual success, rearing at least six young in four consecutive summers; four ospreys were reported from Glenfeshie in 1898 and a pair was still attempting to nest at Loch Loyne. One might dare say that, in 1900, there were unlikely to be less than ten ospreys in Scotland in that summer and there could possibly have been double that number. As there are no grounds for supposing that persecution increased, why did our Scottish ospreys meet their end so quickly?

After 1850 it seems improbable that, even in the best years, there could ever have been more than forty or fifty ospreys in the Highlands and even half that

Suspicious, a cock osprey looks straight at the camouflaged photographer (Photograph by C. K. Mylne)

figure might be regarded as an exaggeration by some. In any reasonably robust population there must be many opportunities for what may be termed 'outlying' crosses involving plenty of new blood. But when a population is reduced to a remnant, in-breeding becomes the inevitable rule, the chances of any really fresh blood being introduced to the small stock being minimal, if not virtually non-existent. Persistent in-breeding, year after year, might well have an adverse and cumulative effect. When, in the earlier decades of this present century, our relict population of red kites had been reduced to a few pairs that bred (or tried to breed) in a small area of Wales, it was widely supposed, although actual proof was lacking, that the comparative lack of success of the few pairs which were not molested was the result of persistent in-breeding. We shall probably never know whether this was a major factor in the swift decline of the Scottish ospreys, ending in their sudden extinction.

In 1893 the Zoological Society of London presented silver medals to two persons who had endeavoured to safeguard and encourage the ospreys to breed in what was, put bluntly, an otherwise hostile environment. The medals went to Donald Cameron of Lochiel and John Peter Grant of Rothiemurchus 'in recognition of the efforts made to protect the ospreys in their respective districts'. It is, perhaps, a little ironical that probably among Fellows of this Society, there were a few who could scarcely be accused of being backward in harrying birds of prey, including ospreys. In perspective, taking a cool and perhaps rather critical view, it might even be asked just what were the steps taken by the recipients of the medals to safeguard ospreys on their respective domains. Judged solely by present values, maybe, it might not seem to add up to very much, but once again, we must not fall into the error of applying current standards to events that occurred almost a hundred years ago. It is not only possible but highly probable that the majority of proprietors of grouse moors today regard themselves as upright, law-abiding citizens and perhaps some hold judicial positions in which they strive to do their duty to their Sovereign and country by ensuring that law-breakers get their just deserts. Yet that diabolical instrument, the pole-trap, is still set to kill birds of prey even today, more than seventy years after it was outlawed by an Act of Parliament. For twenty-five years almost all birds of prey have been protected by law and some, including the osprey, are given special legal safeguards by way of severe penalties for those who choose to ignore them. Yet still many of our birds of prey are deliberately and wantonly destroyed by means of traps, guns and poison. However, the climate is changing for the better, albeit slowly. Many land-owners and others are considerably more broadminded and tolerant than their forebears. Legislation has its uses but it is public opinion which is really effective, although public opinion, particularly if it develops into a crusade led by some flag-waving fanatics, can often become intolerant and sometimes hysterical, too. Sport and conservation were wedded long ago but it is as well that both parties to the union should never forget that any successful marriage demands a good deal of give and take on both sides.

The recipients of those silver medals of the Zoological Society of London were more than worthy of their awards. They were pioneers. That their efforts ended in failure does not detract one iota from the respect in which they should be held. John Peter Grant of Rothiemurchus and Donald Cameron of Lochiel are two names that must not be forgotten in the long history of Scottish ospreys, not least because their abiding interest in birds helped to pave the way for better things to come.

My recollection is that nobody thought very much about ospreys between the two World Wars. It was a tragic story but the osprey had been driven out of Britain and my impression is that few serious ornithologists ever expected that it might nest again. Probably few cared very much, one way or the other, but one or two certainly did. In 1929 Captain C. W. R. Knight obtained four ospreys from the United States and released them at Loch Arkaig, hoping that they might form the nucleus of a new British breeding stock. This effort was a complete failure and as these birds belonged to a different race, some 'purists' may rest more easily in their graves because the experiment foundered. However, the idea was good, although had the imported birds nested successfully they would soon have attracted the attention of the egg-collectors, perhaps a few gunners, too. The ospreys had gone and I rather think that most ornithologists in the 1930s more or less resigned themselves to the idea that they had gone forever.

Even then, of course, there were plenty of stuffed specimens and skins of Scottish ospreys preserved in many museums and private collections, as well as many clutches of *bona fide* Scottish-taken eggs. The stuffed birds, as well as the eggs that, given a bit of luck, might have had the good fortune to become stuffed birds themselves, mostly still exist to testify to the harsh facts. As Richard Meinertzhagen so rightly said, Man is the greatest predator of them all.

CHAPTER THREE

Ebb-tide

Along with glorious birds like the avocet and the black-tailed godwit and the white-tailed sea-eagle, the osprey had been lost to posterity, not through natural causes but through the greed and narrow-mindedness of the collectors. The decline was probably accelerated by the attitude of the landowners on the majority of the large estates. Using shotguns, traps and poisons, keepers waged a constant battle against all birds of prey, from the noble golden eagle down to the tiny merlin. Any creature that might conceivably interfere with the welfare of birds, notably red grouse, blackgame and ptarmigan, which would provide good sport in due season was a prime target and the consequent slaughter, even if we accept that the figures were sometimes exaggerated, is an ugly blot on the history of one of our greatest field sports and one which has provided a lot of enjoyment, as well as employment, for several generations.

Nature conservation has made such enormous progress in the last thirty years that younger readers may be unaware of the situation that existed even up to the time of the Second World War. Although the Royal Society for the Protection of Birds was founded (as the 'Fur, Fin and Feather Group') as long ago as 1889, for very many years the Society had small support, was financially poverty-stricken and lacked the expertise it can command today. Those few who laboured so hard and unselfishly to succour an infant that has grown into a giant did so either for love or for a pittance. Many regarded them as little better than a bunch of sentimentalists, a charge that was probably not wholly groundless. The young society was helped little by the ornithologists of the time;

the history of ornithology is as much tainted by misdeeds and narrow-minded indifference as is the history of shooting for sport. The senior ornithological body in this country, the British Ornithologists' Union, far from giving any practical help to the RSPB, made no serious attempt to decry the activities of oologists, although insofar as rare species such as the osprey were concerned they, above all others, must have been able to appreciate the abysmal results of this crazy and largely unscientific persecution. It is all too easy to take for granted the considerable degree of co-operation and understanding that exists today between bird-conservationists, landowners, sportsmen and others, forgetting that less than fifty years ago those relatively few who were interested in birds were divided into several groups, all largely at loggerheads with one another.

Although it has only come to be appreciated comparatively recently, the problems of bird-conservation are as much international as national. If the osprey had been driven out of Britain early in the present century, it was, like a lot of other rarer birds, faring badly elsewhere. Almost throughout Europe the species had been decreasing. In the Mediterranean, at the southern end of its range, a fairly healthy population was in decline, which was understandable in a region where almost any bird, whether edible or not but the bigger the better, was regarded as 'fair game' by most of the shooters. By the early 1950s it was estimated that the total of breeding ospreys in the Mediterranean had been reduced to about ten pairs.

If this was depressing, it might be argued that it did not directly affect the chances of the osprey ever re-establishing itself in Great Britain, because it is only the ospreys that nest in the northern part of their range which are migratory. Even in the period between the two World Wars there was at least a modest stock of nesting ospreys in Scandinavia. These birds moved south to the Mediterranean and beyond in the autumn and those that survived returned to their breeding grounds early in the spring. On their twice-yearly migrations it was not surprising that a few of these ospreys passed through Britain, being sighted both on the coast as well as at some of the larger inland waters, where they might dally for several days, especially during the more leisurely autumn passage. Rare as they were, these ospreys turned up most frequently in the south-eastern quarter of England but odd birds were seen elsewhere, including Wales and Scotland. If most ornithologists had resigned themselves to the loss of British ospreys, there were one or two optimists who dreamed that, one fine day, one of these birds returning to Norway in the spring might settle for the Scottish Highlands, although it would still have to secure a mate. Evidence suggests that, in the 1930s, the odd osprey may have summered in Scotland.

Unfortunately, during that period the Norwegian ospreys were still subjected to a fair amount of persecution, being sadly and somewhat stupidly regarded as detrimental to the interests of fishermen. Anyway, so long as this downward trend in the Norwegian breeding population continued, the prospects of the birds re-establishing themselves in Scotland appeared less and less likely.

In 1946, immediately after I was 'demobbed' from the RAF, I joined the staff of the Royal Society for the Protection of Birds, becoming responsible for the organization and management of its bird-reserves. I had scarcely settled into this exciting job before avocets, those elegant black-and-white wading birds that had been driven out of England more than a hundred years before, settled to nest at two sites in Suffolk. During the first two or three years, when it was touch-and-go as to whether or not the avocets would manage to sustain this small salient, they occupied a great part of my time. So it was not until 1949 that I was able to plan a long trip into Scotland, including the Orkneys and Shetlands where the RSPB employed a number of part-time wardens in several important areas. It was towards the end of June of that glorious summer that I had the good fortune to meet Desmond Nethersole-Thompson for the first time.

Desmond was surely the greatest field-ornithologist of my generation. As a young man, like many ornithologists of that era, he had collected eggs but his passionate interest in birds was both deep and abiding. Even before I joined the RSPB I was aware of his reputation, but it was not until I met him that I really appreciated his skill and knowledge. When he turned up, late in the evening, at the small hotel at Coylumbridge at which I was staying for four or five nights, his warm-heartedness came through with his handshake. Desmond was a big man—and not just physically, either. For some years he had been employed, very much on a part-time and poorly-paid basis, as the RSPB warden in that neighbourhood in which many rare and uncommon birds nested, including golden eagles, peregrines, crossbills, crested tits and greenshank, as well as dotterel and snow-buntings on the high ground. With Desmond as my guide, the next few days were as enjoyable as any I have ever had in the field.

Among many other ornithological matters, we discussed the success of the avocets in Suffolk. Here was a species that had not nested in England for a hundred years. Although the number of pairs were still very few and all concentrated on one small site at Havergate island, I was confident enough to say that I was fairly sure that the avocet had been regained permanently, barring some awful catastrophe. Desmond's enthusiasm was as obvious as it

Close-up of an adult cock osprey
(Photograph by John Murray)

was genuine. Inevitably we discussed the possibilities of some other 'lost' British breeding birds returning in the future, such as black terns, ruffs and black-tailed godwits. I was rather taken aback when Desmond suggested that we might see the osprey breeding again in Speyside. He told me that in recent years the occasional osprey or two had been 'summering' in the area, rightly adding that all that was necessary was for two birds of opposite sex to meet up early enough in the spring. However, when I pressed him for any further information he gave me very little. As this was the first occasion on which we had met I certainly don't blame him, yet at the time his vagueness left me with the impression that he was probably exaggerating his case. I was sceptical about the prospects and my enthusiasm failed to ignite.

However, that brief trip to Speyside—the first of many—taught me a lot. The importance of the area, ornithologically, had been made very obvious to me. One way or another during the summer months, Desmond Nethersole-Thompson had been expected to cover an area of several hundred square miles and to locate the nests of rarer species, as well as doing what he could to safeguard them from plundering egg-collectors and other perils. Hitherto he had had to rely on his bicycle or his own two feet to get around, unless he was lucky enough to hitch a lift to some of the more distant outposts of his empire. At least I succeeded in persuading the Council of the RSPB to provide Desmond with a motor-cycle (second-hand!) which pleased him greatly and must certainly have made a difficult assignment that much easier.

My concern was not for the ospreys that might return to nest in Speyside but for the broader protection of birds throughout Scotland. Apart from a few part-time or honorary wardens in the Orkney and Shetland isles and Desmond Nethersole-Thompson looking after a large slice of Speyside and the adjacent mountains, the RSPB had no other footholds in Scotland.

My first meeting with George Waterston was in Edinburgh in 1947, when I attended a week-end conference organized jointly by the British Ornithologists' Union and the Scottish Ornithologists' Club. He had rapidly made his influence felt in ornithological circles and in 1936 had helped to found the Scottish Ornithologists' Club. During the war, he was captured in the battle of Crete and was a POW in Germany for two and a half years. In 1948 George bought Fair Isle and established the Fair Isle Bird Observatory—one of the most important bird-ringing stations in Europe. When I met him he was employed in an old-established family business—obviously a square peg in a round hole.

Like many organizations centred in London, the RSPB had tended to

Indulging in vigorous wing-flapping exercises before leaving the eyrie
(Photograph by Jack Dermid/Bruce Coleman Limited)

overlook what went on in distant places. At that time the Society's work in Scotland, as well as in other important districts, might be described as rather parochial. By 1949 I had it firmly in my mind that, at least insofar as Scotland was concerned, this situation should be rectified as soon as possible. After I had met George once or twice I was sure, if the Society could get hold of him, that he was the right man for the job. In confidence, I discussed my ideas with him and was not surprised by his enthusiastic response. Unfortunately the RSPB was a small society in those days, with only four or five thousand members, so that lack of funds throttled my hopes for several years. However, it was not long before George became Hon. Scottish Representative of the RSPB and, although at first he was only working in his spare time, this was a step in the right direction. George knew Desmond Nethersole-Thompson and fully appreciated his remarkable ornithological abilities. I arranged an early meeting in Edinburgh between the three of us. George and Desmond seemed to get along well together. With Desmond looking after Speyside and George able to visit landowners, keepers and stalkers over a much wider area, the prospects for rarer breeding birds of the Highlands had certainly been improved.

CHAPTER FOUR

Alarms and Excursions

There was no further news of ospreys. I had almost forgotten about them when, in 1952, I became Secretary of the RSPB, succeeding Robert Donaldson, a gentleman in the best sense of that word who had faced a long, painful and fatal illness with remarkable courage. By this time George Waterston had proved a wonderful ally and I was anxious to engage him as a full-time member of the RSPB staff, as its Scottish Representative with a small office located in Edinburgh. George was eager to undertake the job, but unfortunately the funds of the Society were limited and, impatient as I was, I realized that the idea must be shelved for the present.

I also continued to take my annual midsummer trip to the Highlands and islands of Scotland which enabled me to keep in touch with Desmond who was able to get around his extensive and difficult terrain much more efficiently than in the past on his motor-cyle equipped with side-car. At the end of each summer I looked forward to receiving his report for the season. It appeared that there was no change in the osprey situation on Speyside during the early 1950s: odd sightings of apparently summering birds—always singletons—were noted, but there was nothing to suggest either that the birds might be nesting or even that breeding might be imminent.

However, I am sure that we all appreciated—none more than Desmond himself—that the district south of the river Spey as it runs down from Kingussie to Grantown-on-Spey was highly suitable osprey country. Bounded on the southern side by the glorious *massif* of the Cairngorm mountains it included the whole of the pine forests of Rothiemurchus, Glenmore and Abernethy, as well as dense forestry plantations. Apart from the Spey itself, there were in this area numerous lochs and lochans, many of them in secluded places, which could collectively sustain several pairs of breeding ospreys without detriment to their huge stocks of fish, both game and coarse. Yet if one had any grounds for suspecting that a pair was nesting, searching for the eyrie in this type of country would be like seeking a needle in a haystack.

However, if Speyside was of great importance the rest of Scotland, representing a very much larger area, was clearly more important still. In 1954 a situation arose in which the flourishing Scottish Ornithologists' Club needed a salaried part-time secretary. Here was the opportunity to make better use of George Waterston's invaluable services and I seized it. The SOC and the RSPB agreed to share George's salary. He was to work on a fifty-fifty basis for both parties, spread over the year as a whole. As the SOC required rather more than their share of his time in the autumn and winter and the RSPB the greater share in spring and summer, this arrangement worked well. The National Trust for Scotland, for whom George's wife, Irene, was working at that time, generously helped by providing office accommodation. I would have preferred to have had George working full-time for the RSPB yet I was delighted with this development as I believe that George was too. It proved to be the stepping-stone to what we both ultimately wanted.

There were difficulties and these gave rise to a certain amount of heart-searching. The finances of the RSPB, as I have already mentioned, were limited. The Council of the Society were unwilling to agree to the cost of employing both George and Desmond Nethersole-Thompson. Speyside, however important, was less vital than Scotland as a whole. In these circumstances it was agreed that Desmond's services would not be retained after the end of the summer of 1954. With the benefit of hindsight, I am still of the opinion that that decision was the right one. Desmond's confidential report on the birds of Speyside in 1954, full of information as it was, made no reference to ospreys. Had he chosen to include in that report all that he knew about ospreys in the area he covered for the Society, the RSPB would surely have made every effort to retain his services. This would not only have prolonged a friendship that I had come to value greatly, but it would probably have made it possible to re-establish breeding ospreys in Speyside long before the end of the 1950s.

George maintained a bush-telegraph among Scottish ornithologists that was second to none. He fed back reports of summering ospreys that began to spark

Putting on the airbrakes
(Photograph by C. K. Mylne)

A Scottish osprey family in 1967
(Photograph by C. K. Mylne)

my imagination. The avocets were now breeding in Suffolk in considerable numbers. A few black-tailed godwits were nesting in the East Anglian fens. Was the osprey to be the next lost species to be regained at last? It turned out to be many months before we got wind of any developments.

It was not until the end of the summer of 1955 that George, unexpectedly, got a positive lead. A bird-watcher from Newcastle-upon-Tyne, by the name of Huntley, had been holidaying in Glenfeshie in June. Understandably he had spent some of his time exploring the splendid tracts of country around Loch Morlich in Glenmore. Morlich is one of the biggest lochs in that area and over 1,000 feet above sea-level. Near the north-western corner of the loch there is a narrow road that climbs up over the Sluggan Pass and on downwards to Strathspey. This road is only about four miles in length and passes through some thick coniferous forestry. It was here, just to the south of the summit of the pass, that Huntley watched a pair of ospreys carrying sticks to an embryo nest. All this occurred towards the middle of June. The eyrie, although not especially conspicuous, was fairly close to the road and could be viewed from it at one point, although it would probably never have been noticed had the activities of the two ospreys not attracted the attention of the observer. We subsequently found out that ospreys are not particularly shy birds and will put up with a good deal provided they are not subjected to deliberate, wanton disturbance.

Huntley, understandably, was bowled over by his astonishing discovery and was well aware of its ornithological importance and the desirability of ensuring that it should not be made public. He was apparently unaware of the fact that Desmond Nethersole-Thompson was no longer employed as a warden by the RSPB and duly sought him out to report the details of his discovery before returning to Newcastle. Desmond was under no obligation to pass this information on to the RSPB and did not do so. As it happened it made no difference.

It was not until several weeks later that George Waterston, in a roundabout fashion, received enough information to send him driving hell-for-leather up to Aviemore. He had no difficulty in locating the eyrie, which was not really much more than a tentative apology for the real thing. If he had hoped to find a pair of ospreys feeding a nestful of well-grown young he must have been bitterly disappointed, for it was the end of the summer and there was not even a sign of an adult bird. There was, however, no doubt about the authenticity of the builders. Following some years of the flimsiest rumours, here was the first tangible evidence that a pair of ospreys had been active in Speyside, even if, at that time, we had no idea why they failed to breed successfully. George told me that he was thrilled to bits when he first set eyes on that nest. I was cock-a-hoop when he told me and was buoyed up with the notion that, the very next summer, we should have ospreys breeding successfully in the Highlands. It was, however, vital to keep the whole matter from becoming public; apart from Huntley and Nethersole-Thompson, only a handful of folk knew what had happened.

George Waterston immediately got in touch with the local laird, Lt Col J. P. (Iain) Grant, whom he knew well. Iain Grant, a great sportsman and naturalist, was destined to play a leading role in much that followed and he certainly earned the RSPB gold medal which was awarded to him a few years later. Practical conservation ran in the family, for it was his great grandfather to whom the Zoological Society had presented its silver medal in 1893 in recognition of the efforts he had made to safeguard the ospreys that were then still nesting (or trying to nest) on the ruins of the castle at Loch an Eilean.

Although the matter was not, perhaps, of any immediate urgency, I took the first opportunity to travel up to Edinburgh. George then drove me up to Aviemore and showed me the nest in the Sluggan Pass. Apart from some disappointment over its small size, the very sight of it made me as excited as a small schoolboy. George pointed it out to me with the kind of pride that made me think that he might even have built it himself. It was a still, rather dreary, overcast afternoon in autumn, the deep silence broken only by the occasional melancholy strains of a robin practising its fall song; I can still recall how the dullness of the weather tempered my earlier optimism. If only the ospreys had successfully reared their young in this Sluggan eyrie it might have been different but, in some strange way, the small black blob of the nest silhouetted against the grey stratus clouds seemed a forlorn object, something like the stark tragedy of a stillborn babe. Nevertheless the eternal, frustrating rumours had at last changed to something like reality, for here, right in front of our eyes, was proof that a pair of ospreys had at least left their card.

That night George and I were the guests of Iain Grant and his wife at Inverdruie. We were hospitably wined and dined and I think it says a great deal for the enthusiasm and stamina of three men that we all sat up into the small hours discussing the problems and possibilities which lay ahead. It is useless to make plans in a mood of pessimism. All three of us were reasonably confident that the ospreys would return to the Sluggan eyrie in the spring unless they failed to return at all. We had, however, no experience on which to draw.

Prime responsibility for the whole operation would rest with George. In one sense I envied him his job. During the previous six or seven years I had been responsible for the operations that had led to the success of the avocets in Suffolk. For all the hardships and frequent set-backs, the challenge had been tremendously exhilarating and, ultimately, very rewarding. In other ways I did not envy George at all. The eyrie in the Sluggan had struck me as being highly vulnerable to any attack by a determined egg-collector and I had no doubts that collectors would be after the eggs as soon as they got any inkling of the whereabouts of the eyrie. The tallish conifer, in which the nest had been built, was situated in the heart of extensive close-planted forestry. It would have been comparatively easy for a collector to approach the tree, completely hidden from any watchers, late in the evening, lying doggo overnight and making his final assault as soon as the light was good enough. If he could scoop the booty and make his escape into the trees before being intercepted, he would be unlucky to be caught.

Iain Grant's enthusiasm that evening convinced me that George held at least one ace in his hand. Maybe it was the blood of his great grandfather flowing in his arteries, but Iain gave me the impression not only that it would be a point of honour to ensure that any nesting ospreys must never be molested but that he, personally, would shoot any egg-collector who dared to climb the tree and he was no mean shot with a rifle. I was somewhat relieved to be assured that he would do no more than put a bullet in the villain's leg!

There was general agreement that it would be imperative to have some sort of hide, providing the best possible view of the eyrie from which the sentries could keep watch. This hide would need to be close to the Sluggan road, yet concealed from it so as not to attract any attention from passers-by, casual or otherwise. Unfortunately we had no idea of how a pair of ospreys would be likely to react. All we could do was to seek some sort of a compromise between having the look-out so close to the eyrie that the birds might be put off, yet not so far distant that it would make it impossible to intercept an intruder.

It was lucky for us that the Sluggan eyrie was situated on Forestry Commission ground because, in matters of conservation, the Commission has a wonderful record of co-operation. Iain generously undertook to arrange the construction of a wooden hide, from plans to be submitted by George, without any financial support from the RSPB. As any tentage in that place would be far too conspicuous, it was important not only that the hide should be large enough to accommodate two watchers, but that there should be room for a camp-bed and a stove on which hot drinks could be brewed. Even in the Highlands, during the first half of May, there are several hours of darkness, especially so if the sky is overcast.

I knew that George would have plenty of other work to cope with during the coming winter which was probably just as well. That Sluggan Pass eyrie would not be out of his mind for long. There was, after all, no certainty that the ospreys would return in the following spring; even if they did, they might nest elsewhere. Waiting in hope is always an anxious business and the nagging doubts tended to increase rather than diminish as the weeks dragged by. There were, however, one or two significant happenings during this period. The first was the almost immediate discovery, purely by chance, of a big nest of sticks in a stunted pine growing in an area of marshy ground close to the southern shore of Loch Garten in the forest of Abernethy. George took me to see it for the

Another osprey family with a fish in the eyrie
(Photograph by E. Murtomaki/The Natural History Photographic Agency)

first time one quiet autumnal day. There was no doubt whatsoever that the ospreys had been there. Compared with the wretched little bundle of sticks in Sluggan, this eyrie was an enormous structure. Ignorant of the habits of ospreys as I was, it immediately struck me that this nest might well have been used more than once. Some of the sticks used in the making of it were very big, two or three feet in length and an inch or more thick. All these timbers were solidly bedded down in depth, conveying the impression that the structure would stand up to any winter gales without suffering much damage.

When had this nest last been used? How often had it been used? What had happened to the eggs or young birds? These were the sort of questions that ran through our minds, although we could only make the wildest guesses at

Hen osprey feeding her chick
(Photograph by Joe Van Wormer/Bruce Coleman Limited)

the answers. Obviously it would have been easy for anybody to climb this small tree and rob the birds of their eggs, for the eyrie was only about twenty feet above ground-level. The place was very secluded and the eggs could have been plundered in broad daylight with little risk of anybody being any the wiser.

We feasted our eyes on the bare bones of this eyrie, not only because it signified that ospreys had been there but that they had more importantly been in business, successful or otherwise. A pair had bred or attempted to breed here at least once. Even at the time I can recall that the size of the nest gave me the impression that it must have been used in more than one season. Both George and I felt that we had stumbled across another pair of ospreys. I am quite sure that, at the time, it never occurred to either of us that there might have been a link between this eyrie and the embryo nest that had been built only a few months earlier in the Sluggan Pass several miles distant and on the other side of a ridge of hills.

George would need to keep a sharp eye on this Loch Garten eyrie when spring came around, yet our main efforts were still focused on the Sluggan. In due course I heard that the wooden hide overlooking the Sluggan eyrie had been completed. George had told me that it was first-class, an opinion which I was able to endorse when he took me to see it early in the following March. We reckoned that we could not expect the ospreys to arrive before April, so we still had a few weeks to wait. It is only accurate to say that George's plans, by subsequent standards, were rather rough and ready. Having no experience to go by and with no certainty that the ospreys would come back, there was little option other than to play the whole thing by ear.

Almost immediately we were hit by a bombshell. On March 26 a letter appeared in *The Scotsman* written by Desmond Nethersole-Thompson. Desmond reported that in 1954 his son had located a pair of ospreys in July and ultimately found the nest from which the young successfully flew. Here was the first reliable evidence of the successful nesting of ospreys in the Highlands for forty years. The writer of the letter, understandably enough, gave no hint regarding the whereabouts of the eyrie, although it was reasonable enough to conclude that it was almost certainly in Speyside. I felt pretty sure that this letter referred to the eyrie at Loch Garten. It was possible, of course, that the Garten eyrie might have been built and used by the birds in an even earlier season. Anyway, two young had apparently been reared in 1954; although it would be several years before these young, if they survived, would reach maturity, they could at least be reckoned as potential Highland breeding stock in future years.

Once we knew that ospreys had bred successfully in the summer of 1954 it seemed much easier to explain the existence of the big eyrie at Loch Garten which George and I had first seen in the autumn of that year. If the ospreys had bred successfully at Garten in 1954 then, unless one of the pair had failed to survive the winter, surely they would have returned to the same area in the spring of 1955? So we reckoned at the time, not unreasonably in the light of subsequent experience. What had happened to the birds in 1955? If, as seemed highly probable, this was the nest which Nethersole-Thompson's son had discovered in July 1954, surely a watch would have been kept to see if the ospreys returned to it in the following April? Did the birds rear young for the second year running? Were they overtaken by some disaster? In his letter to *The Scotsman* Desmond remained silent on this point. At the time both George and I concluded that there were probably two pairs of ospreys trying to breed in Speyside in 1955. The first pair, at Loch Garten, might have been successful; the pair that had built the small eyrie in the Sluggan we knew had abandoned their attempt. The Sluggan pair, so we reasoned, might have contained one bird which had not quite reached maturity, a false notion which helped to raise our hopes that they would shortly return to build up the eyrie and make good use of it. In the meanwhile George made up his mind to keep a sharp eye for any developments at the Garten site.

All George's plans had been made around the Sluggan eyrie. Even those plans were pretty sketchy and if the birds returned, the watching arrangements, at least for the first few weeks, would be largely a matter of improvisation. We had all kept very quiet about the ospreys, knowing that any publicity, even by word of mouth to close and trustworthy friends, might result in some leak that would attract over-enthusiastic bird-watchers who, unintentionally but none-theless effectively, might cause enough disturbance to the nesting birds to bring about a disaster. I do not care to think what would have been our position had we found it necessary to safeguard two pairs in that summer of 1956.

We did not then know that a pair of ospreys which have attempted to breed and met with disaster during the long period when the eggs are being incubated will shift to another site and spend several days building an embryo nest before abandoning it. The nest in the Sluggan, on which for so many months George had concentrated his attention and on which we had focused all our hopes, was, beyond doubt, nothing more than one of these 'frustration' eyries, built by a pair of ospreys only after their first attempt at breeding had failed, probably in the latter half of the five-week period between the laying of the eggs and the hatching out of the chicks.

Loch an Eilean Castle—the historical nest-site
(Photograph by C. K. Mylne)

CHAPTER FIVE

Summer of Frustration

At the beginning of April 1956, the few of us who were involved in what we had privately nicknamed 'Operation Osprey' were not only agog with excitement but our hopes were running high. We still regarded the Sluggan eyrie, overlooked by its splendid capacious new hide, as our trump card. Not one of us had seen a Highland osprey at an eyrie, yet we reckoned we already knew something about them when, in reality, we knew next to nothing. I was busy in my London office but ready to travel north at short notice to lend a hand. The hunt for the ospreys really depended on four people: George Waterston, as the C.O., would spend what time he could spare, mostly at week-ends, concentrating on the Sluggan site but giving some attention to the big eyrie at Loch Garten; Iain Grant was a busy man but he spent a good deal of his time outdoors and it was unlikely that any osprey would cross his path unnoticed; one or two other local people who could be trusted to keep their mouths shut were also on the look-out, as well as keeping their ears to the ground in order to follow up any likely clues.

Concentration on the two known eyries was inevitable because the whole area of mid-Speyside in which a pair of ospreys might otherwise choose to nest was far too large to be adequately covered by our limited resources. George had his offices in Edinburgh and it took him three hours to drive up to the scene of operations. He had been equipped with a Dormobile, so that at least he carried his sleeping accommodation with him. On week-end forays he was often accompanied by his charming and devoted wife, Irene, who is an ornithologist in her own right. Provided that a pair of ospreys returned either to the Sluggan or the Garten eyrie, there seemed no reason to suppose that we could not put up a good showing. Maybe our hopes ran higher than common prudence should have dictated. I waited eagerly, if somewhat impatiently, for George to telephone me with the good news that I was sure would be forthcoming.

In the event, the hide at the Sluggan eyrie turned out to be a white elephant. Nothing happened there in April or early May to raise any hopes. It remained completely deserted. The same depressing situation prevailed at the big eyrie at Loch Garten. In retrospect there is no doubt that we failed to appreciate the magnitude of our task, mainly due to our ignorance of the habits of ospreys. When they first arrive on their chosen breeding-ground the birds are almost as elusive as will o' the wisps. Until close to the time of the hen laying her first egg they may only be on or in the vicinity of the eyrie for comparatively short periods each day. Neither bird of a pair may put in an appearance between the noon of one day and the dawn of the next. Even after the eggs have been laid and the female spends the greater part of her time incubating the eggs, it remains extremely difficult to find an eyrie in any thickly wooded area. The chances of meeting a male bird during the brief period when it might be fishing either on the river Spey or in one of the many lochs and lochans in the area were almost negligible.

Towards the middle of May, George, with nothing to show for his efforts, was understandably both frustrated and bitterly disappointed. There were rumours of the odd osprey being seen in the Rothiemurchus area, nothing more. As it was imperative to make every effort to discover the whereabouts of the ospreys if, indeed, they were nesting at all, I decided, after consultation with George, to send a member of the RSPB staff up to Speyside for ten days or a fortnight. I chose George Edwards, who was our cine-photographer at the time. He was a gritty Yorkshireman with a rich sense of humour which enabled him to laugh his way through all sorts of adversities. Even more important, he was a competent field-ornithologist—every successful bird-photographer has to be. I was reluctant to take him off his main job at the height of the season but I had no choice.

Now that we had a man on the ground our hopes rose again. We should have realized that one man on such a large beat, using his two flat feet to get around, would have had only the remotest chance of finding an osprey eyrie at a time when the eggs would have been in the nest and the activities of the adults at their lowest. At the end of ten days, George Edwards had nothing to report. He had concentrated his attentions on the forests of Glenmore and

A peaceful lakeside eyrie
(Photograph by M. D. England/Ardea, London)

Rothiemurchus. I recalled him so that he could continue with his photography before it was too late. None of us knew that every night when George had retired to well-earned rest in the little hotel at Rothiemurchus, a pair of ospreys were nesting within two miles.

The situation was bitterly disappointing. As May drew to its close it became obvious that either we or the ospreys had missed the proverbial bus. Early in June, just when our spirits were at a very low ebb, there was unexpectedly good news. George Waterston telephoned me in London to report that a pair of ospreys had begun building their eyrie in a tree close to the south-eastern corner of Loch Morlich. Thrilled to bits, I took a train up to Aviemore. George met me at the station. The birds were still busy at the eyrie. We were able to watch three birds flying around in the vicinity of the embryo eyrie although, anxious not to put them off their job, we kept at a discreet distance. The third bird appeared to be an intruder, often chased off by one of the pair, only to return again after a few minutes. We thought that this might have been an immature bird and if we did not altogether approve of his disturbing tactics at what we all fondly believed was a critical stage in the breeding-cycle, we took some heart from the idea that the supposed juvenile might come back to breed next summer. This was the first occasion on which I had ever had the good fortune to watch ospreys in the Highlands and for the very first time I was able to enjoy one of the greatest sights in the bird-world: an osprey fishing for his food. The hover, the steep plunge, the enormous splash which gives one the momentary impression that the huge bird has sunk forever, followed by the strong but somewhat lumbering effort to get airborne, perhaps with a fish held torpedo-wise, head first, in its strong talons.

Believing that the balloon had gone up at last, George and Iain Grant were hastily trying to muster a scratch team of watchers. Rothiemurchus was, by that time, part of a huge reserve of the Nature Conservancy and their warden, a grand chap by the name of Archie Macdonald, had already offered us most of his spare time. Again our enthusiasm outran our limited experience. We could not have mustered a team capable of maintaining a round-the-clock watch over the following five or six weeks. In the event, this did not matter. After a day or two of feverish activity the efforts of the ospreys became more and more desultory as the days passed until, by the end of a week, they hardly visited the eyrie at all and did no further nest-building. Perhaps this was the sort of thing that had happened at the Sluggan eyrie in the previous June? It was all inexplicable and terribly frustrating so far as we were concerned. We resigned ourselves to the bitter fact that the osprey account was closed for at least another year.

The account was not closed, however. Not very long after the ospreys had finally abandoned the Loch Morlich site the BBC, in one of its programmes, announced that a pair of ospreys had nested in Rothiemurchus Forest. We

With the fish still held torpedo-wise, an osprey pauses on a branch
(Photograph by Nigel Charles)

were even indulged with a fairly good recording of the alarm cries of one of the adult birds. These had apparently been obtained by Desmond Nethersole-Thompson, who had been lent the necessary equipment by the BBC. In this broadcast Desmond recounted what was really a most extraordinary story, even if it had a tragic ending.

The ospreys had built their eyrie within about half-a-mile of Desmond's home at Whitewell, close by the river Druie and in the heart of Rothiemurchus Forest. Yet I got the impression that the eyrie was not discovered until some time after the eggs had been laid, which only goes to show how difficult it can be to locate a pair of nesting ospreys in the early stages of the breeding cycle. I believe it was Desmond's young daughter who first found the eyrie. Unfortunately the eggs were apparently destroyed by a marauding crow. In summer a good many walkers are about in that neighbourhood and the ospreys may have been disturbed, however unwittingly, long enough for a crow to seize its chance and seal the tragedy. I have never had much time for crows, but since that disaster in the summer of 1956, I have cherished something of a loathing for the brutes!

Now we were able to hazard a fairly safe guess that the sudden appearance of a pair of ospreys at Loch Morlich towards the middle of June had not been merely fortuitous. There could surely be no doubt that two of the three birds which had been present (and these would have been the two which indulged in nest-building for a few days) were the pair that had lost their eggs at their eyrie in the heart of the forest, only three or four miles away. This was again a half-hearted attempt at a 'repeat' nest, yet it was too late for the pair to have any chance of rearing young. All we had to show for our efforts was little enough: a slightly better knowledge of the breeding habits of ospreys, especially of their behaviour after a first nest had failed; some idea of the kind of site they favoured for their eyrie; the magnitude of the task that confronted us which had at first seemed beguilingly simple; two complete failures and a splendid look-out post in the Sluggan Pass that had never been put to any good use and was unlikely to be of value in any future campaign.

We still had a lot to learn, yet the bitter disappointments had at least taught us something.

CHAPTER SIX

See them—see them not

At the end of the summer of 1956 it was time to take stock. We had little enough to show for a considerable expenditure of time, money and effort, so that it was important to consider our plans for 1957.

During that autumn of 1956 George and Iain Grant put their two wise heads together to good purpose. Early in the New Year I travelled from London to Edinburgh by sleeper and then went on by road with George to Speyside, where, for two days, we were to be guests of Iain Grant and his wife at Inverdruie, Rothiemurchus. I well remember that I had a bedroom which looked out over the forest to the distant *massif* of the Cairngorm mountains and my excited delight when I woke up as day was breaking and saw the hills, deeply-covered in snow and glowing pink beneath a glorious sunrise backed by a lucid blue sky. The Grants were wonderful hosts but the main purpose of our visit was to discuss plans to protect the ospreys when they returned in the following April. George was in one of his best 'but me no buts' moods, so that any suggestion we discussed on what to do *if* they returned was answered with a derisory snort!

George's view, supported by both Iain and myself, was that it was useless to wait until we had definite news that the ospreys had been seen in Speyside. Once they had settled in, finding the eyrie would be largely a matter of luck. The first essential, therefore, was to have one person who would be resident in the area before the ospreys could be expected to arrive. Such a person should be a skilled ornithologist, available for at least several weeks. The accommodation problem was quickly resolved by Iain Grant. He was willing to refurbish a crofter's cottage and so we all went out to have a look at it. This was Aultnancaber, about one mile from Coylumbridge on the road that runs up to Loch Morlich and Glenmore Lodge which, in those days, was rough and unmetalled and carried little traffic even in summer. It was a pleasant spot, as well as being secluded, admirable for our purposes. This generous offer of the cottage, which really was a godsend, did a lot to boost the morale of both George and myself.

The next difficulty was to find a reliable ornithologist who would be willing to undertake a long and arduous stint and who could be implicitly trusted to keep his mouth shut. This man, apart from hunting for ospreys throughout the greater part of the day, would need to be an early-riser because his best chances of running down the quarry would be highest around sunrise or during the two or three hours thereafter. Either he would need to breakfast in the dark or undertake at least two or three hours of hard reconnaissance before he took his first meal of the day. He would also have to make himself *persona grata* with a number of important local contacts and have enough commonsense to keep a sharp eye open for any suspicious-looking characters, for there was little doubt that the egg-collecting fraternity, certainly the greatest if not the only threat to the ospreys, was as much aware of what had been going on as we were ourselves.

George Edwards was no longer available and I had nobody in the small RSPB staff at London headquarters whom I could second to the job. George Waterston, too, was engaged in many ploys. However important they were, the ospreys were not the only rare birds in Britain at that time. Luckily I remembered an old friend, Guy Brownlow. Guy had been a regular soldier, a sapper officer who had retired from the army a few years after the end of the Second World War. He was a great enthusiast for birds, common or rare, and had been of great assistance as a voluntary watcher guarding the avocet colony on Havergate Island in Suffolk. He was a bit of a 'loner', a bachelor who lived on his own, so that a spell at Aultnancaber would suit him down to the ground. April and even early May can be both bleak and stormy on Speyside but I knew from experience that Guy was a tough, tenacious character.

A pair of ospreys on their substantial eyrie
(Photograph by James Tallon/The Natural History Photographic Agency)

As soon as I returned to London I got in touch with Guy Brownlow and was not the least surprised when he leapt at the assignment. So I put him in touch with George and the final plan of campaign was worked out. Our strategy was simple enough. Guy was to travel up to Speyside and take up residence at Aultnancaber early in April. His job would be to hunt for any signs of an osprey in and around the forests of Glenmore, Abernethy and Rothiemurchus, keeping an especial watch in the vicinity of the old eyrie, still in good condition, in the marsh beside Loch Garten, and the 1956 eyrie in Rothiemurchus. Apart from that, Guy would have a free hand. Any sightings of ospreys would be reported to George Waterston in Edinburgh. If a pair were located either at an old eyrie or building a new one, both George and I had agreed to down tools and make a dash up to Aultnancaber and assist Guy in watching the eyrie site on a rota basis. Iain Grant offered to lend a hand with the night-shifts, until such time as we would establish some sort of a camp well to the rear of a look-out post and muster a team of reliable volunteers who would see the operation through to what we were all determined should be a successful conclusion. This would probably mean sustaining the effort at least until the end of July but the critical period would occur whilst the female was incubating her precious eggs, a space of about five weeks which we reckoned would occur between mid-May and the end of June.

We were well aware that the biggest threat to a pair of nesting ospreys would be posed by skilled and determined egg-collectors and if there was no shortage of these peculiar gentry, one successful looter would be sufficient to wreck all our efforts. Yet there were other hazards, all the more worrying because we had little experience of the behaviour of ospreys on which to base some sort of judgement as to what might be prudent and what foolhardy. In our efforts to safeguard the nesting birds we should have to be careful to avoid any disturbance to the ospreys; if we had to make an error it had better be on the side of over-caution. The birds might also be inadvertently disturbed by bird-watchers, walkers and others approaching the vicinity of the eyrie. There were also too many crows in Speyside for our peace of mind. Whilst we reckoned that under normal circumstances ospreys could probably be relied on to see any marauding crow off the premises, if the birds were disturbed by anyone, crows might well seize an opportunity to swoop on the eyrie and pillage the precious eggs, as had happened in the summer of 1956.

By that February of 1957, such plans as we could reasonably make were brought to a conclusion. None of the few of us involved underestimated the difficulties, least of all George Waterston, who had to continue to bear the chief

Male osprey in threat display
(Photograph by C. K. Mylne)

responsibility for the whole business which, following war-time precedents, had now been officially dubbed 'Operation Osprey'. There were, however, at least six weeks of waiting before there was any likelihood of anything happening. During this period we had to be optimistic, if only because a third successive failure must surely jeopardize the whole future of the Scottish ospreys, yet at the back of one's mind the nagging thought kept intruding—had the ospreys already shot their bolt? There were, of course, some moods of great optimism when we wondered what we should do if we found *two* nesting ospreys on our hands, with perhaps one pair using the eyrie at Loch Garten and the other in Rothiemurchus Forest. The Garten eyrie had withstood the winter very well; it was a massive affair and looked to me much the same as when I had first set eyes on it two years earlier. The Rothiemurchus eyrie, however, had almost disappeared.

Guy Brownlow set course north from his home in Suffolk early in April in a sturdy but rather aged red van which was not particularly fast. He called in at the RSPB offices in Edinburgh for a final conference with George Waterston and arrived at Aultnancaber on April 7. The cottage there had been almost transformed by Iain Grant. The living-room-cum-kitchen now boasted a carpet over its rather chilly stone floor, it had been furnished and there were sufficient rooms and enough beds and bedding to accommodate two or three people in reasonable comfort. The outside 'privy' had been fitted up with an Elsan, and most supplies, including milk, were obtainable from the little store at Coylumbridge, which was only a bare mile down the road. We did not expect the ospreys to put in an appearance until the third week of the month but we reckoned that Guy would need a few days to settle in and find his way about the neighbourhood.

Although fairly compact, it was far from an easy piece of terrain and, furthermore, Guy was a stranger to it. As the osprey flies it was only six or seven miles from the site of the previous year's eyrie in Rothiemurchus to the one at Loch Garten, but by road it was a different proposition. Rothiemurchus and Glenmore Forests are adjacent but Abernethy Forest, in which Loch Garten is situated, is separated by a line of hills, from Craiggowrie (2,237 ft) in the north-west to Meall a'Bhuachaille (2,654 ft) in the south-east. It was possible for Guy to get his van, by road and rough track, a good deal of the way to the Rothiemurchus eyrie but they might choose to nest anywhere in that forest and a good deal of hunting on foot would be necessary. There was some suitable nesting habitat for ospreys right away to Glenfeshie, a distance of several miles, but it was agreed that Loch an Eilean, with its historic associations with the birds, marked the western boundary of our searches. By taking the rather rough and sandy road eastwards from Aultnancaber to Glenmore Lodge it was possible to get a good view of Loch Morlich. It was only a couple of miles from Morlich, along a narrow but serviceable road, to the summit of the Sluggan, where the 'frustration' eyrie had been built in 1955. There were thus three areas, all reasonably close to Aultnancaber, that needed watching.

We may have been semi-hypnotized by the massive and long-standing eyrie at Loch Garten, yet we all believed that this might prove the best bet. Unfortunately it involved the longest journey. The quickest way to reach it was by dropping down to Coylumbridge and then taking the road past lovely Loch Pityoulish, the round trip not far short of twenty miles.

It must be remembered that spring comes late to the Highlands. There are usually few signs of it until May when the ubiquitous birches start to leaf and the primroses blow. Even in that month the higher hills are often deep in snow and lying snow on the lower ground is not exceptional even if it does not linger long. Aultnancaber is itself around 900 feet up. The weather in April is usually more typical of winter than spring, especially so at five or six o'clock in the morning when the skies are clear and the wind blows from the north or east.

The hen keeps guard, perched on the rim of her eyrie
(Photograph by C. K. Mylne)

Most birds are usually far more active in the early hours of the day and again, to a somewhat lesser extent, towards evening and ospreys are no exception. It was a good thing that Guy Brownlow was, by habit, an early riser. In order to arrive at the Garten eyrie before sunrise he had washed (in cold water!), dressed, breakfasted and was on the road by four o'clock, as often as not either in bitter, wintry weather or with rain pouring down.

It was tough going and physically wearisome. Guy subsequently told me that he often snatched only a light breakfast, drove to Loch Garten, arriving before sunrise and then spent four or five hours watching the deserted eyrie and the surrounding marsh either from the screen of trees east of the eyrie or from a more distant vantage point to the west, on the rough track which runs from Garten up to Loch Mallachie. Arriving back at Aultnancaber around noon, having done his daily shopping on the way, he would cook himself his first real meal of the day. Once that was washed-up he would either go prowling in Rothiemurchus or spend some hours watching Loch Morlich and the Sluggan

Pass areas. Sometimes he mustered enough energy to return to Garten before sunset, keeping watch until twilight and only arriving back at Aultnancaber after darkness had fallen. He then set about preparing his main meal of the day, knocking back a stiff dram of malt whisky during the process and then washing his dinner down with a glass or two of wine; he never saw any objection to mixing grain and grape!

It was hard going and the regular routine became monotonous as day succeeded day without any sign of an osprey. Guy told me that after the first week, although he began his day's hunting in a buoyant mood of optimism, by the time the evening came he often felt tired and depressed. All on his own, I could understand it when he added that it was only listening to his radio for an hour or two late at night that saved him from going round the twist.

However, at least Guy Brownlow was *doing* something. George Waterston and I, fretting our hearts out in Edinburgh and London respectively, had nothing to do but wait for some good news. I daresay George, who had been responsible for almost all the careful planning over many months, suffered more than I did but, if so, he has my deepest sympathy. There was nothing at all that we could do until an osprey, preferably a pair, put in an appearance.

No news is often said to be good news; in the case of Operation Osprey it was quite the contrary. George Waterston had planned to spend the whole of the long Easter week-end up at Aultnancaber, thus not only providing Guy Brownlow with a bit of relief as well as good companionship but making it possible simultaneously to have a watcher in the Rothiemurchus-Morlich area and the more distant Garten site.

It was one of these ironical twists of fate that Guy was not the first person to see an osprey in Speyside that spring. On the Sunday preceding Easter Day an ornithologist, J. Baird, was in the Loch Garten area, not apparently looking for anything in particular, when he was both surprised and delighted to watch an osprey carrying a large stick in its talons. The bird took the stick to the old eyrie and after fitting it into the big structure, sat on the nest for several minutes before flying off. Guy was at the site later in the day but saw nothing of the bird and therefore had no reason to suspect that at least one osprey had turned up at last. So the birds were back after two years of failure!

There was, to be precise, only one bird, but as we knew that males usually arrived at the breeding sites a few days before their mates there was no cause for concern. It was also known that a lone male would renovate the eyrie in a desultory manner. My guess is that the bottle of malt circulated fairly freely at Aultnancaber on that Good Friday evening!

If our general strategy had been worked out months earlier, tactics had to wait until battle was about to commence. In all the seventeen years during which I served the RSPB I never met anybody who, given the spur, could galvanize himself into positive action either as quickly or with as much enthusiasm as George. The Loch Garten eyrie, upon which most attention was now to be focused, was situated on the Seafield Estates and on the day after his arrival George motored over to see the factor—perhaps Easter Saturday is not the most suitable day to do business with anyone but needs must when the ospreys drove. George was welcomed with genuine enthusiasm and he was virtually given *carte blanche* to take any steps which he might consider necessary to safeguard the birds. This co-operation continued throughout many years and the ultimate success of the Garten ospreys owes much to it.

The Garten eyrie was situated in a stunted, rather dead-looking pine in a piece of marshy ground immediately to the south of the loch, perhaps half-a-mile in length and half that distance across from east to west. The north margin was the loch itself; on the east it was bounded by thick, coniferous forest that came down to the very edge of it; to the south the ground rose, at first very slowly but then a little more steeply, to the Mains of Tulloch; to the west was Loch Mallachie from which a rough track ran back, mostly through more forestry, to join the Boat-of-Garten–Nethybridge road.

There was not much traffic on this road although even in those days, on fine week-ends in summer, it attracted small parties of picnicking motorists and their children. The eyrie, however, was a full mile distant from this road and could not be easily seen from it, being only about twenty feet above ground level even though built almost at the very top of the stunted pine. The slightly rising ground to the south of the eyrie tree was very much more open but it was a wild bit of country, unlikely to attract visitors. The eyrie could be viewed from the track which ran up by Loch Mallachie but this was only used by the odd forestry worker. The best and by far the most secluded prospect of the eyrie was obtainable from one point where the thick forestry edged the marsh on its south-eastern margin. As a viewpoint it also held the advantage over the Loch Mallachie track in being closer—about two hundred yards from the eyrie.

Characteristically, George took no time at all to make up his mind, now that it seemed probable that the ospreys would use this Garten eyrie, that Aultnancaber was too far away to be used as anything more than a convenient base camp to which any watcher, if he could be spared, could retire from the front-line and enjoy a day's comfort and a night's sound sleep. The bit now between his teeth, George dashed off to Grantown-on-Spey and hired a fourteen-foot caravan and, with the aid of his sturdy Dormobile, towed it back to Loch Garten. South of the loch the road to Nethybridge rises quite a bit and at the top there was an extremely rough and boggy track which penetrated for a few hundred yards into the thick forestry, ending in a small clearing. This clearing was scarcely the brightest of spots, being densely surrounded with pine and fir trees. The ground in the clearing was moist and rather peaty, which presumably accounted for the dearth of trees. Except in the finest weather it was a dank sort of hole and when it rained it was positively depressing, although it offered excellent shelter from strong winds blowing from any quarter.

Demonstrating the immense wing-span
(Photograph by C. K. Mylne)

George was not interested in creature comforts. As a camp-site this clearing was almost perfect. The rough track leading to it was disused and the clearing itself quite invisible from the road. Voices in the camp would only carry a matter of yards because of the thick screen of trees in all directions. He had also made a thorough reconnaissance of the neighbourhood before he acquired the caravan and had discovered that a little pathway, barely trodden, ran down to the fringe of the trees at a spot which afforded a well-screened but reasonably close view of the eyrie. I got to know the site only too well and I could appreciate how George had the utmost difficulty in towing the caravan down the rough, wet and rutted track to the clearing. There was no fresh water at the site, so that this vital commodity would have to be ferried over from Aultnancaber each day in a jerrycan, together with other essential supplies. Before the light faded, again aided and abetted by his two willing assistants, George rigged up a makeshift screen of sacking at the end of the quarter-mile path which ran down through the thick forest to where the trees ended on the edge of the marsh. A peep-hole was cut in the sacking so that a watcher, sitting on the cold comfort of an upturned oildrum, could keep a wary eye open for an osprey without the slightest risk of the bird either seeing or hearing him. This screen was wide open to the sky and offered no real shelter from the chilly elements but it would have to serve until the ospreys had settled in. Now that an osprey was known to have arrived at the eyrie and even added a stick or two to the structure everyone was confident that it would not be long before a pair settled in for the season. Then, maybe, a more substantial, weatherproof and comfortable hide might be quietly erected behind the make-shift affair which would have to serve for the present. Thus Operation Osprey had been well and truly launched. The caravan was locked up as twilight settled and the workers returned to Aultnancaber for a well-earned dinner.

There must have been a mood of optimism prevailing over that Easter week-end. It not only seemed probable that the ospreys were going to use the Loch Garten eyrie but, if so, for the very first time we knew of the eyrie that was to be used right from the start, even before the hen had put in an appearance. To maintain a round-the-clock vigil, on a basis of three hours on watch followed by six hours during which to cook, eat, sleep, wash and cope with the routine chores, the minimum requirement was for three experienced, fit and active persons. Including himself, George had a team of three at that time but Patrick Ellis, a young man who had travelled up with him, would be leaving at the end of April whilst George would have to spend some time in his Edinburgh office if only to arrange for a supply of voluntary wardens, all of whom would have to be healthy, experienced and personally known to him. George had problems and no mistake!

The threat from egg-collectors was unlikely to arise (or so we all thought at that time) until the ospreys had concluded their courtship and the female had laid her first egg. As the hen had not even put in an appearance at the end of the third week in April it was a fair presumption that incubation would not start until the second week in May. There was no point in trying to recruit a small band of reliable watchers until the female had arrived on the scene and it had become reasonably certain that the pair were intending to use this Garten eyrie, but some plans had to be made because time was short. The idea of sweating away night and day to safeguard one of the finest of our raptorial birds and watching over a nest which, if our dreams came true, would probably be the only one of its kind in all Britain, may sound rather more romantic than it actually was. Apart from the uncertainty that anything would happen at all, there were still so many difficulties to overcome and resources were far too limited to cope adequately with them all.

Guy Brownlow was a splendid anchor-man, dedicated to the job and prepared to live in the caravan until the end of the summer if required. I think George Waterston had made up his mind that once the ospreys started nesting he would himself see it through until the eggs had hatched—a period of at least five weeks during which he would occasionally drive down to Edinburgh early in the morning, cope with as much urgent office work as best he could and be back on Speyside the same evening. I knew that my colleague in London, Peter Conder, who had taken over the job of running the Society's bird reserves soon after I had been appointed Secretary of the RSPB in 1952, would be as keen as mustard to get in on the affair. When the balloon went up I reckoned that Peter and I could alternate at Loch Garten, each doing spells of ten days or a fortnight. However, it was obvious that this would be inadequate for a spell of watching sustained over five to six weeks.

All were agreed that any determined raid on the eyrie by an egg-collector would most probably be made at night and certainly between sunset and sunrise. It was also agreed that a maximum of three hours was enough for an individual stint, for nobody could be expected to keep absolutely on the alert for longer. The two most difficult watches would be that immediately before midnight and the following one, when it would be dark or, at best, deep twilight for much of the time. As summertime was already in force midnight was not until one o'clock, watch-time.

George planned to return to Edinburgh on the Easter Monday and set about trying to rustle up some volunteers who, in pairs and bedded down in hired tents, would come to Garten in relays once the ospreys had laid-up, staying for a week or a fortnight and thus raising our strength to five persons. The two 'outsiders' might well be inexperienced and the idea was that they would cover the four three-hour watches between 7.0 a.m. and 7.0 p.m. They would each do two spells of watching but both would be in broad daylight during which the only disturbance was likely to come from casual intruders, so far as the birds were concerned.

This arrangement would leave the three 'key-men' to cover the four watches between 7.0 p.m. and 7.0 a.m. With four watches and three watchers, by taking the stints in strict rotational order, each watcher would be involved in taking different times for three days, when the sequence would repeat itself. The watcher who went on at seven o'clock in the evening would have to take a second turn between 4.0 a.m. and 7.0 a.m., but, apart from the fact that he would be able to get himself a supper after he came off his first stint and snatch at least four or five hours sleep before going on duty again, in both his periods he would be working in daylight or near-daylight which would obviously be much less demanding than constantly peering out in deep twilight or even darkness, alert to the slightest sound that might betray the presence of an intruder in the vicinity of the nest. The two night-watchmen who only did one stint of three hours each would also have to be responsible for cooking, shopping in Boat-of-Garten and other camp chores so that, apart from catching up with much-needed sleep, they were unlikely to find themselves with much spare time on their hands.

I had always shared George's anxiety that, during the darkest hours, it was not really adequate to have only one watcher on duty at the hide. We could only guess at what might happen if a determined raid were made at night, but it might be that more than one person would be involved. Even if there were only one intruder the watcher might be hard-pressed to prevent him from getting away with his plunder if he were a powerful man. Nobody was frightened of getting hurt but it would be a poor consolation for a broken nose if a collector and his ill-gotten booty had vanished without trace. The rough-and-ready look-out post was fully four hundred yards from the camp site and with the dense screen of trees intervening, the loudest shouts for assistance from a watcher at the hide would never be heard, even supposing anybody in the camp was wide awake.

This dense afforestation was useful because it completely blanketed any noise and laughter at the camp—even the watcher on duty in all the stillness of evening could seldom hear a sound—which meant that there could be no disturbance to the ospreys, but it had its drawbacks. The answer was to have two watchers on duty at the hide for the two shifts on either side of midnight but manpower would not run to it. It was going to be difficult enough to maintain our minimum of five watchers over the next several weeks.

In all the discussions and the anticipatory bustle of that Easter week-end there was only one fly in the proverbial ointment. Although there was much to do at the camp site and a return was made to Aultnancaber to get a night's rest as soon as twilight began to fall, the eyrie was watched by one of the three men throughout a good portion of the daylight hours without the osprey putting in an appearance. The lone osprey had been missing for over a week. Could Baird have been mistaken in his sighting of that single osprey on April 14? It is probable that, as one blank day succeeded another, such doubts did cross the minds of those who lay in wait, yet an osprey is not a difficult bird to identify and, anyway, what other bird would carry a stick in its talons in the immediate vicinity of an eyrie? Baird's record was good enough for any pessimistic doubts to be short-lived. Besides, these were early days. The lone male (and it almost certainly was a cock, although it is impossible to be absolutely sure) was generally assumed to be hunting around over a wide area in search of a female, a guess that was probably as good as any and helped to sustain morale. In bird protection, as with many other things in life, to lose hope is to lose the game, set and match.

George Waterston returned to Edinburgh on the evening of Easter Monday, leaving Guy Brownlow and Patrick Ellis—the latter due to leave fairly soon—to comb the area for any signs of ospreys but concentrating on the Garten eyrie. I had been out of touch for several days but George telephoned me the next day and briefly outlined his plans. It was then that I promised him that either Peter Conder or myself would somehow or other be available as watchers during the long, critical weeks when the osprey was incubating her eggs. Although he had a lot on his plate Peter, not unexpectedly, was 'rarin' to go' and made immediate plans to travel up to Speyside. Already we were beginning to be haunted by the notion that the osprey which had put in one appearance at Loch Garten had, in fact, found a mate and the pair might already be building a nest in the deep forests of Glenmore or Rothiemurchus. If Peter, with his great experience, could get up to Speyside without delay it should be possible both to keep a sharp watch on the Garten eyrie and also to spend long hours combing other likely areas, especially in the vicinity of the eyrie in Rothiemurchus in which eggs had been laid in the previous year as well as around the 'frustration' eyries in

Two ospreys in their Loch Garten eyrie, a view familiar to thousands (Photograph by C. K. Mylne)

the Sluggan Pass in 1955 and on the edge of Loch Morlich in 1956. We were all tremendously excited and if the scent was abominably 'catchy', at least the hounds were questing with noses very close to the ground.

The day after George Waterston had left for Edinburgh, Tuesday, April 23, Guy Brownlow was at Loch Garten late in the afternoon, entering the makeshift, cramped and uncomfortable hide at 4.30 p.m., determined to keep watch until after sunset. An upturned, empty oildrum is not the most comfortable object upon which to rest one's bottom, especially when one has to stay in a fixed position, peering out through a narrow slit in a hessian screen. Guy stuck it, however, for two hours during which he saw nothing. He then took a stroll through the forest for half an hour to ease his cramped limbs before quietly returning to watch out the last two hours of daylight. It was a fine, sunny evening, very welcome after a spell of stormy weather but the hide faced the north-west and the setting sun made watching especially difficult, even somewhat painful, at this period of the day. However, Guy had hardly settled down before he received a thrilling and well-earned boost. He spotted a large bird of prey wheeling around in dark silhouette against the brilliant sky. It did not come to the eyrie tree but he had several views of it and had no doubt that it was an osprey. So the bird had returned after an absence of nine days. It was still only one bird but the sight of it was enough to recharge the batteries, so that Guy was back in the hide again at four o'clock the following morning, not long after dawn had broken.

Throughout the mornings the light was behind the watcher and this was always the most favourable period for viewing the eyrie tree. It was unfortunate that a screen of smallish trees—birches and pines—dotted about the marsh completely obscured the base of the low pine at the top of which the enormous nest had been constructed. During this early morning watch Guy was rewarded with several brief views of the osprey circling round. He must have been chortling with glee after long days of frustration and around eight o'clock the bird came and perched on the edge of the eyrie itself, alternating spells of preening with long periods when it simply stood and did nothing. Eventually it took to wing and disappeared and, although the watcher waited for some time, it did not reappear.

Guy Brownlow drove back to Aultnancaber at his best speed which, in my experience, was a highly dangerous one. He picked up Patrick Ellis, loaded supplies in his van and then returned to Loch Garten to establish themselves in the caravan.

Guy subsequently told me that the presence of the osprey at the Garten eyrie for some while on the previous evening and again for an hour or more on the following morning convinced him that the birds were going to use the old eyrie, even though, so far, only a single bird had put in an appearance. He did not telephone the good news to George, because George was due to pay another flying visit to Speyside at the week-end. So neither George nor I, biting our finger-nails in frustration, knew anything of the return of our osprey prodigal.

After the morning visit the osprey did not put in an appearance in the afternoon, although watch was maintained until it was too dark to see. The Thursday was even more frustrating. Although an almost continuous vigil was kept throughout daylight hours, not only from the hide but also from more distant vantage points affording a wider view, the bird was not sighted.

Enthusiasm, however, still ran high. Guy was up early on Friday, April 26, and was in the hide before sun-up. This time he had not long to wait. Around five o'oclock he was elated to observe the osprey flying round and then alighting on the eyrie. Apart from a few short flights when it disappeared from view, it remained on the eyrie for two hours. All this was especially encouraging because this was easily the longest period the bird had so far been known to remain on or around the nest. Although the bird did not return again for the rest of the day, the watchers got the impression that, at long last, things were really beginning to warm up. It should be remembered that Guy Brownlow had already been on the job for nearly three weeks and had had little return for his pains.

It was at about this time that Peter Conder joined the team. The hopes of the watchers were somewhat dampened when the osprey once more failed to appear on the Saturday and then raised again when it returned on Sunday, April 28. At least it seemed to have some sort of a 'fixation' for the Garten eyrie but, with April drawing to a close, the absence of a second bird became increasingly disturbing. The rest of the 1957 story was pure anti-climax. The osprey was not seen on either of the last two days of April and then made a brief appearance on May Day. Then it disappeared completely. Although one man kept a sharp watch at Loch Garten, the other scoured Glenmore and Rothiemurchus throughout one day after another. It was wearisome, fruitless work which simply had to be maintained but it was inevitable that the first mood of optimism was slowly replaced by a tired pessimism. As day succeeded day it was obvious that time was running out.

Out of the blue, as it were, late on the evening of Monday, May 6, the osprey was back on the eyrie. Surely there was still time . . . If only it found a mate! After two more days of absence it was again seen flying around the loch for a short period but it did not come to the eyrie nor was there any sign of a second bird. Three more days of energy-sapping frustration were followed by the reappearance of the bird on May 13, when it visited the eyrie for a few minutes. It was at about this time that Peter Conder returned to London and, as Patrick Ellis had already left, Guy was left on his own. Even George Waterston, whose enthusiasm was almost limitless, was becoming pessimistic and to save expense the camp site was closed and the caravan was towed back to the hirer. Guy returned to Aultnancaber but continued to concentrate on the Garten eyrie. After being absent for two days, the osprey was back on the eyrie for several hours on Thursday, May 16. It was never seen again that summer.

CHAPTER SEVEN

The Balloon Goes Up

Operation Osprey, proudly named when our hopes were running high, was developing into a nightmare. One way and another, the omens could scarcely have been less propitious for 1958.

George began to lay his plans in the autumn of 1957. Iain Grant once more placed the Aultnancaber cottage at our disposal. This would be the initial base for the operations and the choice of a first-class 'anchor man' was an essential ingredient to the success of the operation. Guy Brownlow had served us well. However, he had slogged it out for the better part of three months, mostly working solo, and it seemed unfair to approach him again. I was once again able to help in this vital matter. I had first met Group Captain R. C. (Bob) Dawkins during the War and we had subsequently become good friends as a result of a common interest in birds and hill-walking. Bob was a quiet, capable character who could not only be trusted to do the job to the limit of his not inconsiderable ability but, equally important, he could be relied upon to keep his mouth shut; in operations of this kind a chance word let slip in the wrong place can all too often breed a mint of trouble. I went down to see Bob at his home in Newton Blossomville, Bedfordshire. Having sworn him to a cut-your-throat, cross-your-heart pledge of secrecy, I was delighted when he accepted, but whether I was more delighted than he was I would not care to say.

One reliable enthusiast who, six months and more before his services would be needed, was both able and willing to assist Operation Osprey for anything up to three months in exchange for nothing more than rough board-

and-lodging got the 1958 planning off to a good start, yet it was fortunate that there were many months available before our schemes would have to be put into practice. It will help the reader if I explain that, in planning his broad strategy and tactical details in advance, George was wont to base them on the presumption that the ospreys would make use of the eyrie at Loch Garten and in our many discussions I fell in with this approach. It was not as silly as it might sound.

We knew that in 1956 the ospreys had built and used an eyrie in Rothiemurchus Forest, at least ten miles from Loch Garten. However this nest, along with the 'frustration' eyries, had long since disappeared, leaving only the solid structure at Garten as a firm focal point around which we could spin our web of ideas.

The ground on which we had concentrated, broadly consisting of the forests of Abernethy, Glenmore and Rothiemurchus, embraced some thirty or forty square miles of difficult country and already stretched our resources to the limit and beyond. George, who made uncommonly few mistakes in this tricky business, was absolutely right in regarding it as an act of folly to extend our area of search. By this time it was more or less an open secret that ospreys were attempting to re-establish themselves in that part of mid-Speyside around Aviemore and Nethybridge and it was there that our efforts to protect them should be concentrated. If ospreys were nesting in some distant location then egg-collectors, bird-watchers and photographers would be just as unlikely to know of their whereabouts as we would be ourselves.

Early in the winter, when there was already some snow lying on the high hills, I was in Edinburgh and George drove me up to Speyside in his Dormobile in which we were able to enjoy a good sleep overnight. The next morning, much as a moth is attracted by a light, we went up to Loch Garten and spent most of the day there. The ground was so wet that we left the vehicle beside the road and walked down the track between the tight-packed fir trees to the clearing where the camp had been, the deep ruts made by old manoeuvrings of the Dormobile and caravan brimful with water. Except under a high summer sun it was never a particularly pleasant spot and now it seemed peculiarly dank and cheerless. I agreed with George that in spite of certain shortcomings it seemed the best spot for a base camp if the ospreys nested at Garten, if only because it was completely isolated.

We strolled down through the firs and pines to the look-out, a few bits of hessian still clinging to the rough uprights, flapping idly in the chilly breeze. I suspect that we were both relieved when we peered out over the marsh and saw

The 1958 eyrie at Loch Garten
(Photograph by C. K. Mylne)

that the big eyrie was still intact at the top of the low, lone Scots pine. It would be simple enough to patch up the rough hide, come the longed-for need. We were still convinced that the only real threat to the successful breeding of a pair of ospreys, excluding natural causes over which we could not exercise any control, lay in a determined raid by an egg-collector. This was no idle threat, either, because a nice clutch of well-blown, 'home grown' osprey eggs tucked away in a cabinet was a prize which would be regarded by most collectors as ample reward for the time, skill and the risks involved.

We walked out over the marsh to have a close look at the eyrie tree. The eyrie, to our great relief, seemed as strong and robust as ever, its huge sticks firmly interwoven and likely to stand up to any storms at least as well as the half-dead pine in which they had been placed.

The eyrie tree at Loch Garten was not the one which would have been chosen from the many available by those protecting the birds. Once a foothold was secured on the lowermost branch (which admittedly was not all that easy), it was almost as simple as walking upstairs to reach the eyrie itself. We discussed the obvious advantage of sawing off two or three of the lowest branches long before the ospreys were due to return. Even if that were done it would still be possible for any determined egg-collector to scale the tree and reach his booty by using climbing-irons but it would take longer and create more noise, alerting the watcher on duty even if he could see nothing and giving him more time to reach the tree and intercept the intruder before he had pouched the eggs, let alone made his getaway into thick cover. There was, of course, no certainty that one watcher, even if he did reach the base of the tree whilst the plunderer was still up it, would come off best in any subsequent maul if his 'opponent' were a physically stronger and younger man. There was no point in pretending that safeguarding the ospreys would be a gentlemanly, kid-glove affair.

Our lack of experience of the osprey's habits was one reason why it was decided not to interfere with the tree. There was a risk that the male osprey on his return in April might not find the eyrie to his liking if he found more than half the live boughs had been lopped off, although they were not ones in which he had ever been known to perch. The last thing we wanted was to take an irrevocable step that might cause the birds to abandon this particular site. It seemed best to leave well alone.

There was another factor to be borne in mind. The eyrie tree at Garten was already half-dead and as it was much favoured by the ospreys we hoped that it would survive for years as a nesting site. If we removed at least half of the live branches there might be a danger of hastening its decay.

It was for much the same reason that George discarded the idea of chopping down a score or more of the saplings, mostly birch, between the eyrie tree and the look-out hide on the edge of the marsh. The temptation to do this was strong because it would have enabled the watcher to see the ground within a radius of some twenty yards of the foot of the eyrie tree and any intruder, even if he were crawling on his belly, might be spotted long before he was in a position to make his final assault. Given the benefit of hindsight I think George will agree that we should have cut some of the lower boughs and cleared some of the scrub to widen the field of view, but we did not know then that ospreys are nothing like as 'touchy' as we feared they might be.

George had made his decisions on a number of points that must have been worrying him for months. Practice is always so much more valuable than theory. At the end of the day, it all came down to the nagging subject of manpower. George had already arranged for an option on a caravan. The demand was not high in April and May, so that an immediate hire would be available. It was considered that the fourteen-footer used the previous spring was really too small and an eighteen-footer had been earmarked. It had been decided to beg, borrow or hire at least six tents of a size adequate to sleep one person in modest comfort. These would be equipped with ground-sheet and sleeping-bag. We had discovered a strong-flowing spring within a hundred yards of the camp site. This was a welcome windfall. The water was clear and although it tasted foul and was quite unsuitable for drinking even if boiled, it would be ideal for washing purposes. Except in an emergency the big caravan would not be employed as a dormitory; it would be used for cooking and eating meals in at least some comfort, as well as providing a place where off-duty watchers, if they were not engaged in some other task, could talk or read or write the odd letter.

On the now accepted basis that no watcher, except in an emergency, should be required to concentrate for more than three hours before being relieved, there would be eight spells in every twenty-four hours. It was going to be much easier to enlist volunteers from among the older age group. Physically fit, retired men, even if they were in their late sixties, could fairly be asked to undertake two daylight stints each day, so that two persons would be sufficient to cover the watching between 7.0 a.m. and 7.0 p.m. although bearing in mind the many camp chores and the maintenance of our supply-lines, three would be better. The risk of any real trouble in full daylight was surely slight.

Our anxiety lay in the four watches falling between 7.0 p.m. and 7.0 a.m. It was the two watches on either side of midnight (1.0 a.m. BST) that worried us most. Whilst it was absurd to ignore the possibility of a daring raid being made on the eyrie in broad daylight, George and I were agreed that the periods of greatest danger would be around last light and first light and of these two we regarded the latter as by far the most threatening.

A skilled egg-collector might arrange to be dropped by car at last light on the road up by the Mains of Tulloch, work his way carefully up to within fifty or a hundred yards of the eyrie tree under cover of darkness and then lie up in thick cover through the day, making a dash for his booty at last light. If he were successful in pouching the eggs and getting out of the tree before being intercepted, the gathering darkness would certainly assist him in making his escape to some place where a car would be waiting to pick him up.

A large chick in the eyrie, while the male osprey perches lower down to the right (Photograph by C. K. Mylne)

Nevertheless, a raid by a collector at last light could involve a sustained effort lasting over twenty-four hours, including at least twenty during which he would have to lie up in boggy ground, more or less prone and immobile, plagued by flies and probably subject to exhausting attacks of cramp. On the other hand if he dared to risk trying to get into a hiding-place near the eyrie tree during the three or four hours before sunset, he would not only expose himself to the obvious danger of being spotted either by some native well-disposed to us (and most were) or an off-duty watcher enjoying a healthy stroll along the Mallachie track or on the higher ground about Tulloch where there were fair views down the long slope and over parts of the Garten marsh itself.

At least two, frequently three persons—youngish, fit and absolutely reliable—would be required to cover the two critical night watches. This was not really enough, however. If all went well it would be vital to sustain our effort, day in, day out, for several weeks. It was necessary also to insure against possible sickness. Even an ailment as simple as a bad cold might render one of the night-duty team unfit for a task that demanded both alertness and physical fitness.

George was neither an optimist nor a pessimist, being about as level-headed as they come. However, he reckoned that in the four months between concluding his plans and the expected arrival of the ospreys in April he would have a fair chance of recruiting a succession of volunteers. I knew from experience, when trying to muster wardens to safeguard the Suffolk avocets, that this was a tricky and often frustrating business. In offering their unpaid services for a week or a fortnight, such people had to sacrifice a part of their annual holiday. It was also important to try to make the right choice, although beggars cannot always be choosers. I also knew that some of these folk, enthusiastic enough when invited well in advance, were all too apt to change their minds, sometimes at the last moment. But George had enough worries and it was none of my business to add to them, so I kept my mouth firmly shut on this point.

What about the three youngish, fit and experienced lads we needed for the critical night and the first daylight watch? Bob Dawkins was one. He would be in the operation from the very outset and had undertaken to carry on at least until the chicks had hatched out—even for longer if it were essential. George and I planned to alternate, overlapping a bit whenever necessary, over periods of not less than ten days at a stretch. We still wanted one more and neither of us could think of a suitable person. It was then that we thought of the Nature Conservancy. The Director of the Conservancy at that time was Max Nicholson.

A cock osprey circling overhead
(Photograph by C. K. Mylne)

In his field, which was a pretty wide one, Max was one of the most able and indefatigable individuals I have ever met. He was a good friend to me during the many years I worked for the RSPB and I agreed to go and see him and try to enlist support. All we wanted was one active warden to be seconded to Operation Osprey for about six weeks—from the time of the egg-laying until the hatch—and as any Conservancy warden was likely to be both a fit man and a conscientious one, it would not be necessary, though naturally desirable, to have the same individual throughout the whole period.

I recollect that Max was greatly impressed when I outlined George's plans in some detail and I had no doubt that he appreciated our dire need. Obviously in May and June most of the Conservancy wardens would be particularly hard-pressed. However, whether it was due to Max's tremendous enthusiasm or my own powers of persuasion—or perhaps a bit of both—he delivered the goods with characteristic generosity and without adding a lot of if-and-buttish riders. Several wardens might have to be used but he promised that one would be with us at Loch Garten (or anywhere else) within forty-eight hours of receiving my request. It was one of the most encouraging things that had come our way for months and, what is more, I knew that Max's word was his bond. We had our vital third man. All we had to do now was to restrain our impatience for three or four months until the ospreys returned.

It was very early in April when Bob Dawkins travelled up to Edinburgh and joined George. They went on together to the cottage at Aultnancaber, spick-and-span and ready for occupation. It would have been absurdly optimistic, judging by the events of the previous year, to expect any osprey to arrive so early as the end of the first week in April but George stayed on with Bob for a day or two, both to show him round the difficult terrain and to acquaint him in some detail of the plans he had made for Operation Osprey, 1958.

I was eager to travel up and join them but as there was nothing useful that I could have done it would have been a waste of time and money. I had a bag more or less ready-packed to take the train for Aviemore immediately George told me that it was considered that egg-laying was imminent. Until then I had to exercise some firm self-discipline. It was not always easy and I confess that there were times, sitting in my office at Eccleston Square in London, perhaps with one ear cocked to the song of a blackbird in the leafing plane trees, when I found it difficult to concentrate on less important matters.

Bob Dawkins had a sturdy motor-scooter for transport. Without neglecting other localities, he had instructions to concentrate on the Loch Garten site, especially early in the morning and again late in the afternoon. His scooter, which was big enough to take a pillion passenger in fair comfort, was just about as fast as a car on the generally twisty roads and much more economical fuel-wise. It was much less conspicuous than a car, easily hidden behind trees or bushes and, moreover, light enough to be driven along any track or ride which was a great advantage. On the other hand the rider was exposed to all weathers. In physique Bob never looked a particularly tough guy but he was as fit as a fiddle and game for anything. In the morning and again late in the afternoon he drove to Garten from Aultnancaber and back either for a snack lunch or for a good dinner in front of a crackling log fire and a hard-earned night's rest. It was routine, unexciting toil and he got his baptism of snow and rain and icy roads.

The first osprey had not been seen the previous year until April 14. The earlier we got some good news the better for our spirits but neither George nor I

Hen osprey alert on her eyrie
(Photograph by C. K. Mylne)

expected to hear anything from Bob much before the middle of the month. However, that time came and passed without Bob having seen a single bird. There was no real cause for anxiety at this stage, yet the lack of any good news was depressing, especially with the fiasco of the previous year still fresh in our minds.

A few days later George telephoned me in London bubbling over with excitement. Bob had been watching an osprey flying around the Loch Garten eyrie. I rubbed my hands with glee, sure in my own mind that this was the male—it almost certainly was—and that he would find a mate in a matter of a few days. If this was wishful thinking I can only say that, at the time, it was essential to be optimistic to retain one's sanity.

A few more days brought the depressing news that the osprey had disappeared from Garten and had not been seen anywhere else. This behaviour was so similar to that of the previous year that it was like a body-blow. However, my own feelings of disappointment must have been slight enough compared with those of George Waterston, who had been deeply involved in his plans for Operation Osprey for months on end. Yet it was still early days and George promised to let me know at once if there were any developments. On each successive day I waited expectantly for a call, but the last week of April passed without any word. It was even worse than it had been in 1957 when, over a similar period, the lone osprey had been seen at Loch Garten at least for a short while about every third or fourth day.

By the end of the first week of May, I had resigned myself to the worst. Unless the ospreys were building a nest elsewhere in one of the forests, in which case it was important to locate them quickly, the whole thing looked like ending in another ghastly anti-climax. Neither George nor I knew that, in fact, Bob Dawkins was working at full-stretch, spending almost every long day at Garten, watching over the marsh from the cover on the Mallachie side and, moreover, watching two birds which were obviously opposite sexes.

The lone male had returned on May Day and hung around the eyrie much of the time. On the third day of the month it was joined by a second osprey and although there was little immediate activity and often both birds took themselves off for hours at a stretch, they seemed to be interested in one another and much attached to the big eyrie. Whilst George and I were nursing our dark thoughts, Bob, after weeks of frustration and weary work, was in transports of delight. He had arranged with George that, just as soon as he was reasonably certain that he had located a pair of ospreys that looked as if they really intended to set up their eyrie home he would send him a telegram containing the one enigmatic word: 'Inflation'. Shrewdly he held his hand until the moment had come for George to put his elaborate schemes into operation which, once started, could not easily be stopped.

Soon the birds started soaring round the marsh and bringing in sticks to refurbish the eyrie, the male fetching most of them whilst the female, who stood for long periods on the nest, helped with the delicate business of fixing them securely into the growing structure. Each succeeding day the two birds spent more and more time in or around the eyrie. On May 8 both birds were around almost throughout, the male bringing in great lumps of moss as well as a few more sticks. Bob did not leave Garten until it was getting dark. It is not difficult to imagine his feelings as he hastened back to Aultnancaber in the gloaming.

The next morning, May 9, he was back at Loch Garten very early and, having checked that both the ospreys were in residence, he scooted off to a post-office to send his telegram. He addressed it to George Waterston at the Scottish Office of the RSPB. Now George, with his responsibility for all the Society's work north of The Border, had many other matters to attend to besides the possibility that ospreys might nest on Speyside. On this particular morning he had to go off early to see a police sergeant in a small place some forty or fifty miles from Edinburgh. In his absence Bob's telegram was opened by his wife, Irene. She knew exactly what it meant and the necessity of getting the message through to her husband without delay. She immediately telephoned the station and spoke to the sergeant. As George had not yet arrived, she impressed upon the helpful policeman that she had just received a telegram and that it was of the utmost importance that George should be given the contents of it as soon as he arrived. The policeman carefully wrote the message down on a piece of paper and promised to pass it on as soon as George came, although one cannot help thinking that he must have scratched his head more than once as he stared at the two bald and cryptic words: 'Inflation. Bob.'

George duly got the message and no doubt cut his business with the police sergeant as short as possible. He then rang me up in my London office and gave me the great news. I could guess from his voice that he was bursting with excitement yet he could not have been more thrilled than I was. We cut out the cackle, however; George informed me that he was returning at once to Edinburgh. He hoped to clear his desk that afternoon but, whether he succeeded or not, he would be off in the Dormobile by evening, heading north with his wife to join Bob at Aultnancaber before midnight. I at once decided to take the overnight train from Euston to Aviemore, where George assured me that either he or Bob would meet me off the train. I undertook to get in touch with Max Nicholson at the Nature Conservancy and ask him for the additional watcher he had promised us. It was unfortunate, perhaps, that all this was happening on a Friday. When I spoke with him, Max was delighted with the good news. However, he felt that, at such short notice, it might be difficult to release a Conservancy Warden in time for him to reach us at Loch Garten over the week-end. This did not unduly worry me, partly because I did not foresee the necessity of round-the-clock watches on the eyrie immediately and partly because, even if such a situation arose, there would be three of us to tackle the job, whilst Iain Grant had already indicated that he would be glad to help out on any night watch, especially at week-ends. So I was more than satisfied with Max's assurance that a warden, complete with land-rover, would probably be with us on the Monday and, at latest, by the Tuesday. After what had seemed a very long time I got the impression that, at last, the tide of fortune was flowing our way.

My own plans were simple and to me exciting. I intended to stay at Loch Garten for about ten days, return to London for a week to clear my office work and then go back to Speyside and, if all went well, remain there until the osprey chicks had hatched out and the long period of anxiety and danger over. That great day might be five weeks or more away, but what a triumph it would be, well worth all the sweat and toil that would probably be involved. I was in a sort of seventh heaven of delight when I boarded my train that evening.

CHAPTER EIGHT

Disturbers of the Peace

My train arrived at Aviemore not long after sunrise. Bob was there to meet me and whisked me back to Aultnancaber on the pillion of his scooter for a welcome breakfast, over which he gave me all the news. Then we were off and away past Loch Pityoulish. It had been a clear night so that although the sun was already quite high a white frost was still clinging to the grasses of the road verges. It was a perfect day for a perfect occasion. On reaching Garten we turned up the Mallachie track and found George and Irene, both as excited as we were, watching the eyrie from behind the screen of their Dormobile, with the new, bigger caravan that George in one of his early-morning fits of zeal, had already towed back from Grantown-on-Spey.

I was not the only one who could not keep my eyes off the ospreys. For long periods they were both on the eyrie. Sometimes the cock would fly around and then return with a stick or great lumps of moss and grass and heather clutched in his talons and then both birds were engaged for some minutes in what looked like rather clumsy attempts to add them to the big structure. Now and then both flew around the eyrie before resettling and once mating took place on the nest. It was a memorable sight and I feasted on it for some time before George dragged me down to earth and he and Bob and I discussed the situation.

I knew that George had thought out his strategy carefully and I had not foreseen that, faced with the reality of the situation, the tactical situation might demand some reappraisal. George was of the opinion that, at least for a day or two, we might be in a better situation if we all remained, as we then were, on the Mallachie side of the small marsh. It afforded us a good, if rather distant view of the eyrie itself as well as a much wider panorama over the surrounding area than any watcher in the old hide to the south-east could possibly obtain. He and his wife could sleep in the two-berth Dormobile whilst Bob and I dossed down in the caravan. We could all have our meals in the caravan and through the windows could keep an eye on the birds and the surroundings whilst doing so. So far as we knew the female had not yet laid her first egg and certainly incubation had not begun. At this stage, therefore, there was no obvious need to start worrying about night watches; so long as we remained alert until darkness fell around ten o'clock and at least one of us was up and about at first light surely no harm could befall the birds.

Even if we took things fairly easily there were still a few jobs to be done. Thus we had to arrange for the loan of a cycle so that we could fetch our drinking water from a friendly crofter's well when we shifted our camp into the wooded clearing. It would also be necessary to lay in some supplies, which meant a trip to the shops in Boat-of-Garten. It looked like being a quiet week-end before we took up action stations and I was well pleased. The morning was perfect, the warm sun having quickly melted the last of the overnight frost. It was almost windless and the bird-music was at its best, innumerable willow-warblers flitting around amid the bright green foliage of the young birches and uttering their falling cadences. It was a wonderful background against which to watch ospreys.

George was always a lad for brewing up a pot of tea on the slightest pretext so that very soon, in the midst of our confabulations, we were all sitting comfortably inside the caravan, blessing our good fortune.

Suddenly somebody shouted that the ospreys were up. We all bundled out of the caravan and watched the pair circling around the eyrie. At least one bird was uttering a high-pitched *pew-pew-pew-pew* call which I soon came to appreciate was an alarm note, used whenever the birds were disturbed. There was no doubt that the birds were disturbed now, yet we could not see anybody and there were no crows around. This was the last thing that we wanted to happen just when the birds were settling in. Then we spotted a figure moving quietly among the thick birches halfway between ourselves and the eyrie tree. George let out an angry yell that could probably have been heard a mile away. The intruder stopped and turned round. We could see that it was a woman. It turned out to be Miss Betty Garden, the daughter of a doctor who lived near Aberdeen. Betty was spending a week-end bird-watching in the neighbourhood. She knew nothing about the nesting ospreys until, picking her way across the

Landing on a dead branch
(Photograph by C. K. Mylne)

marsh amid the dense growth of small birches, she had suddenly seen them flying round overhead. If Betty Garden had demonstrated how a bird-watcher can, however inadvertently, disturb rare breeding-birds, she really could not be blamed for what had happened although it was some time before George was sufficiently mollified to offer her a cup of tea! I knew Betty because I had stayed at her family home a year or two earlier, when lecturing to the Aberdeen Branch of the SOC. She was a sweet person and died in tragic circumstances only a few years later. But she does not enter into this story of the ospreys only as an intruder, for in the weeks ahead she was able to help us on several occasions, coming over to our camp for the day, cooking a meal, tidying up the caravan and generally ministering to a bunch of troops who, as time went on, suffered more than a little from fatigue induced by a marathon effort. Betty will always hold a place in the hearts of those few of us who pioneered the early years of Operation Osprey.

George Waterston was a cheery individual who inspired all those who worked with him. However, when he was perplexed he always frowned. Long after he had forgiven Betty for her accidental intrusion on his sacred preserves and the ospreys had settled down as if nothing had happened, he was still frowning. The incident had clearly perplexed him. If he had reckoned that the view of the marsh from the Mallachie side was a good one, it was now obviously not good enough to ensure that an intruder could not approach the eyrie tree without being seen. We were all a bit shaken but it was a salutary lesson. The incident demonstrated how alert the man on watch would need to be even in broad daylight once the eggs had been laid. If it was unlikely that any egg-collector would attempt to rob the nest in daylight it was clearly feasible for a person to approach fairly closely to the eyrie tree before the ospreys took alarm. However, we now knew that they would probably demonstrate if there were any disturbance close to the nest, at least in daylight: whether they would react in the same manner during the hours of darkness was another matter. Betty Garden had been strolling about without any attempt at concealment: a stealthy approach to the eyrie tree in deep twilight might not alarm the ospreys at all. During the hours of darkness I was pretty certain that ears were going to be just as important as eyes. I was already convinced that, once we got down to the job, any watching from the Mallachie side would be out of the question, if only because the distance from the eyrie tree was much too great.

George's immediate reaction to Betty Garden's unexpected incursion was to have one man on official look-out duty. The fact that, most of the time, we all of us had our eyes on the birds might seem to make this order somewhat irrelevant, but this was not so. George was quick to appreciate that although the ospreys engrossed our attention for most of the time it was still quite possible, if only for a few minutes, for all of us to be occupied by something else. The ospreys appeared to have settled down again as if they had never been disturbed. For most of the morning the bird which we presumed to be the female was either standing on or sitting in the nest whilst the male, perched on a dead branch of a pine nearer the loch, either preened himself or, adopting a somewhat hunched-up attitude, did absolutely nothing.

Well knowing that the time would very soon come when we had little or no time for leisure, the easy tempo of that morning, disturbed only by poor Betty's innocent foray, was enjoyable enough. We had all been up early and as there were jobs to be done during the afternoon, by noon we were ready for a meal. Tea was brewed up and we were all tucking into bully-beef butties when, suddenly and unexpectedly, the ospreys were up and around, screaming in alarm and the look-out man, field-glasses held in one hand and his sandwich

A male osprey hunched up and motionless on favourite perch
(Photograph by C. K. Mylne)

in the other, yelled out that there was another intruder on the marsh. We all spotted the figure of a man. He was not just wandering about but weaving in and out among the birches, obviously making for the eyrie tree. George let out another yell that might have made a sergeant-major on the parade-ground at Sandhurst green with envy. The unknown stranger kept going, not even bothering to look round. George leapt into action. Ordering Bob and myself to get on the scooter and make a dash round to the old look-out on the far side of the marsh, he raced off towards the eyrie tree.

It was an electrifying moment and Bob and I needed no second bidding. I was on the pillion of the scooter even before Bob had started the engine. We roared down the rough track to the road running past the eastern end of Loch Garten in a high state of excitement, then up the slope beyond where I had to get off to open the gate giving access to the primitive, rutty ride which led directly into the clearing where we intended to establish our base camp. There we left the scooter and raced ahead on foot. It was all downhill to the old look-out and, with the benefit of daylight to enable us to avoid surface tree-roots and other hazards, we probably covered the four hundred yards within two minutes.

George had already escorted the stranger off the marsh and was at the old, tattered hide. The intruder, to give him due credit, was as cool as the proverbial cucumber but George was blazing with anger. We gathered that the stranger, who had had a three hundred yards start in a four hundred yard race, had reached the tree, had then climbed it, in spite of George's ferocious yells, and looked into the nest before descending. By this time George had reached the tree and, anxious only to ensure that the ospreys were not disturbed for a moment longer than necessary, had led the stranger off the marsh before telling him, in about the fiercest language I have ever heard, exactly what he thought of him. The trespasser was utterly unrepentant, coolly informing us that there was already one egg in the nest and that if we wished to search him we were at liberty to do so—an invitation which George declined to take up because he had himself reached the foot of the tree by the time this man had reached the top and was quite satisfied that he had done no more than take a swift glance into the eyrie.

When asked by George the stranger gave his name. I pricked up my ears because it was that of a man known to me as an egg-collector who could be fairly regarded as a menace to the safety of the eggs of any rare species one might choose to mention. When George requested his address he refused to oblige. It just so happens that I possess a kind of photographic memory so far as important addresses and telephone numbers are concerned and this enabled me to give George the information he wanted. For the first time since we had had this chap in our grasp, so to speak, he seemed a trifle nonplussed. He refused to accept George's view that he had done any harm by disturbing the ospreys. He declared, in what was then a sort of egg-collector's theme-song, that he never took the eggs of rare species, which I regret to say was a blatant lie but I must add, in all truth, that he stood up to George's blasting with remarkable self-assurance, especially as Bob and I were breathing murder down the back of his neck.

Eventually George enquired how he had got to Loch Garten and he replied that he had his car parked on the road near the Loch. George, who was determined to see the back of him, after telling Bob and me to remain at the look-out at least until the ospreys had settled again, escorted him quickly back over the marsh to his Dormobile. After a few minutes we heard them drive off. The ospreys had gone quiet by now. The female had not returned to the eyrie however. We sat and waited behind our screen of trees, knowing that Betty Garden and Irene Waterston would be keeping a watch on the far side of the marsh, hoping that one of the birds would soon return to the nest. This did happen but not before we had a shock that nearly gave us both heart-failure.

I have already mentioned that there were far too many crows in the area for our peace of mind. There always seemed to be several hanging around, so that we suspected that some of them must have been non-breeding birds. Now a 'hoodie' came into view close to the eyrie, cawed once or twice and then, to our horror, side-slipped and settled on a short dead branch immediately alongside the eyrie which, we now knew, already contained one egg. We jumped to our feet as the bird took a menacing, sideways hop towards the nest and, recking nothing for the peace of the ospreys in this moment of dire need, rushed forward out of the cover of the trees, yelling and clapping our hands. All this, fortunately, was too much for the crow, the bird beating a hasty retreat. It was, however, a remarkable demonstration of the kind of disaster that can so easily overtake rare birds if they are disturbed, however briefly, by a human intruder in the vicinity of the nest.

It was a great relief when, after an interval of several minutes which seemed like a lifetime, the female osprey suddenly appeared from out of the blue, stood quietly on the edge of the eyrie for a short while, obviously very much alert and finally settled down in the cup, apparently incubating her one egg. She kept bobbing up and peering round, obviously still unsettled by the recent outrageous disturbance of her privacy, yet for just so long as she remained on the nest there

A Loch Garten osprey on its eyrie
(Photograph by S. C. Porter/Bruce Coleman Limited)

seemed little real danger from any marauding crows. We considered it best to remain on watch, however, and within the hour we heard George's footsteps as he came plodding down the rough pathway through the firs. We were agog to hear his news.

George had carried out his offer to drive the egg-collector to his car which had been parked beside Loch Garten. This had not been an act of courtesy because, as we had both guessed, George was anxious to get the registration number of the vehicle. Having seen him off the premises, George had driven down to the police station in Boat-of-Garten where, by a stroke of good luck, he found the friendly sergeant at home. No doubt it was news to the police sergeant that ospreys were nesting on his beat but, perhaps rather surprisingly, he showed great interest in the whole matter, listening attentively as George related his story and gave him the number of the collector's car. George considered that it was quite likely that the collector was staying in the area; if that was so, it would be useful to know just where. The policeman said that he would ring up some of his colleagues in the neighbourhood and see what he could do: if George would call back at the station later on in the afternoon he would gladly give him any information he could obtain.

We told George about the crow incident. Whatever action we might take in our forthcoming efforts to guard the ospreys this particular occurrence impressed upon all of us the necessity to avoid, at almost any cost, any disturbance of the ospreys themselves. George had already decided that our time for any lotus-eating was over. It was typical of the man that, in a few brief intervals for thought in what had been a pretty hectic hour-and-a-half, he had already decided exactly what he was going to do. Bob would remain where he was, keeping a wary eye on the nest and, working as quietly as possible, do what he could to renovate the old look-out hide. George had a further supply of hessian in his Dormobile but more elaborate repairs had better be done early on the following morning, when the ospreys had had a chance to settle down. Leaving Bob on guard duty, George and I trekked back to the clearing and then we drove round to rejoin Betty Garden and Irene to give them all the news.

George's plan was to establish the base camp in the little clearing in the deep forest at once. We hitched up the caravan to the Dormobile and, leaving Betty to watch for any developments on the Mallachie side, Irene and I went off with George. It was a tricky business to negotiate the Dormobile and the caravan down the rough track to the road but the going was even harder along the narrow ride through the forest and into the clearing. By the time the job was finished to George's satisfaction the sun was already getting low in the west.

A female osprey comes in to land
(Photograph by C. K. Mylne)

Irene brewed up another cup of tea in the caravan whilst George went off to fetch Betty Garden. As soon as he got back I went down to the look-out and relieved Bob. It was a late afternoon of glorious sunshine, quite warm, too, and I was not sorry to get away from the shady darkness of the clearing. I was a bit 'edgy' after the earlier happenings but nothing occurred to disturb the serenity of my watch although I am bound to admit that, insofar as the ospreys were concerned, it was a trifle boring. The birds changed over at the nest once or twice but, for the most part, I was staring through binoculars at a massive bundle of sticks above which a white head occasionally moved. I was, however, happy enough. In that bundle of sticks, within five or six weeks, a brood of young ospreys would first see the light of day. Given the effort, there was nothing to stop us now.

I suppose I must have been on watch for two or three hours because the sun was sinking low towards the Monadhliaths when George eventually came down to join me, bringing the glad tidings that Irene, the self-effacing power behind the throne, was cooking up a meal that would be ripe for eating within the hour. Better still, George had been down to the police station and had been given the news that the egg-collector's car had been reported travelling, southward bound, through the Pass of Drumochter, past Dalwhinnie and heading for Blair Atholl. Rightly or wrongly, we reckoned we had scared the pants off the blighter. We should not see him again—or should we?

George had borne the brunt of the day's operations and was pretty tired. If the excitement had not been altogether to our liking, there was no denying that it had proved a lively day. We had learnt quite a lot, too. George and I had both retreated to a patch of sunlit heather which gave us a satisfactory if rather more distant view of the eyrie, lay down and lit our pipes. It was all incredibly tranquil, crested and other tits calling from the scattered firs and pines, blackbirds carolling their orisons and a song-thrush singing away up towards the Mains of Tulloch, whilst curlews bubbled out their lays almost incessantly. We were both disinclined to talk much but George, between long intervals of puffing away and occasionally swatting at a biting insect (of which there were plenty) unfolded his immediate schemes bit by bit. With only one egg in the nest he considered it unnecessary to maintain a watch throughout this first night. I certainly did not argue when he suggested that we could all do with a good night's rest. He had an alarm clock and would set it for four o'clock, at which hour it would still be almost dark. He would take the first shift at the look-out, leaving Bob or me to relieve him at seven. After that we would keep watch on a basis of doing three hours on duty, followed by six off, until the Nature Conservancy warden put in an appearance. Perhaps it was the fine weather, the glorious scenery, and the evening choir of the birds that affected my judgement, yet it all seemed delightfully easy to me at that moment.

It was already getting decidedly chilly and twilight was well advanced when we pottered back up to the caravan to enjoy the last first-class meal, with all the company present, that was likely to come our way for some time. Then George and Irene moved over to the Dormobile and Bob and I got ready for our bunks in the caravan. We could only wash if we groped our way by torchlight to the spring in the forest several hundred yards away. We opted for remaining unwashed. There was no fresh water left, either, unless one or the other of us had been game enough to walk half-a-mile with a bucket and knock up a crofter and his wife who had probably already gone to bed themselves. Such niceties were not important in Operation Osprey. We removed our boots, took off our jackets and trousers and lay down beneath our blankets. We needed

A well-camouflaged eyrie, showing how difficult ospreys could be to locate (Photograph by C. K. Mylne)

them too! It was clear and frosty outside, so that long before daybreak the windows of the caravan were thick with condensation.

Writing this almost twenty years afterwards, the events seem almost as fresh as if they had happened yesterday. They turned out to be so different from what I had expected that the passage of time has done little to diminish my astonishment. The osprey vigils became a part of a relentless, unremitting routine. On the Sunday following the dramatic occurrences already described I had arranged to relieve George at the look-out post at seven o'clock. Never having any difficulty in waking before six o'clock I had no need to fall back on an alarm-clock. It was a chilly, grey-looking morning when I woke up, donned trousers and boots and, seizing soap and towel, went out of the vapour-ridden caravan into the chilly morning air, leaving Bob snoring away like a happy trooper. If the birds were singing I did not notice them as I trudged down through the saturated undergrowth to the strong spring that gushed out of the bank of blaeberry and sphagnum. The water was ice cold as I soaped and sluiced my head and shoulders and chest. Wide-awake at last and with my teeth chattering I reckoned that, insofar as washing was concerned, this was more than enough for the time being. Back at the caravan I lit the calor gas and would have put a kettle on except that I then remembered there was not any water. So I finished dressing, left a scribbled note for Bob to fetch some fresh water as soon as he woke up and set off, rather before time, to relieve George at the hide.

George who had enjoyed only three or four hours sleep, was not exactly a ball of fire. When I discovered him in the hide he was sitting on an upturned wooden box which, he assured me, was at least more comfortable than the oil-drum that had been in use previously. After I had had my baptism of three hours sitting on that bloody box my deepest sympathies went out to the whilom oil-drummers. George reported that everything was quiet and that the ospreys, turn and turn about, had been sitting serenely throughout his vigil. I told him about the dearth of fresh water, warned him to make sure that Bob was up in time both to get his breakfast and be ready to relieve me at ten o'clock and then settled down, with a great feeling of pride and satisfaction, to my first tangible contribution to the success of Operation Osprey.

George had provided us with a log-book and a ball-point pen, both firmly attached to one another by a length of string, in which watchers were asked to note down any occurrences of importance.

The wretched little hide of sacking was just about as uncomfortable as anything in which I have ever been incarcerated. It was not only very narrow but the sagging roof was so low that one had, perforce, to sit in a constricted, round-shouldered posture, peering out through a long, narrow gash in the rough hessian which afforded a fair view of the eyrie but little else. The eyrie itself was two hundred yards away but with nightglasses, carrying a magnification of seven times and objectives measuring fifty millimetres, it was easy to see things in considerable detail. However, the top of a stunted, half-dead Scots pine does not offer much variety by way of detail even when it is embellished with a noble pile of sticks constituting the nest of a pair of ospreys. The sitting bird seldom showed more than his or her head and neck, often a good deal less than that. With the field-glasses it was possible to see the eye of the bird, the hooked beak and the white and brown crown feathers but a few minutes of this, apart from making one's arm ache, was enough to satisfy the aesthetic whims of even the most enthusiastic ornithologist. Anyway, a few minutes of sitting was quite enough to make one appreciate that the bare end of an upturned box was confoundedly bad for one's bottom. There was really little point, at least in full daylight, in constantly peering through field-glasses. One simply watched the eyrie with naked eyes, knowing that the sitting bird would give notice of any intruder, scarcely daring to divert one's attention to anything else that might be happening round about.

Eventually the morning mists evaporated and the sun came out. Immediately I perked up and felt all the fresher. If it were almost boringly easy to keep watch on the ospreys by day, inevitably one fell to wondering just what it would be like, working entirely on one's own, at dead of night. My next watch would be from four until seven o'clock in the afternoon, which would also be easy enough. But after a six-hour break I should be due for another three-hour stint. It would be pitch dark then and as it was still quite early in May there was unlikely to be a glimmer of daylight until around three o'clock in the morning, perhaps even later if the sky were overcast. In darkness or near-darkness it would be necessary to watch the eyrie constantly through night-glasses. Prompted by this thought I immediately picked up my glasses and did a really long spell watching with them. I soon began to feel thirsty and not a little hungry and I was glad when Bob arrived promptly for his watch, accompanied by George. George had a roll of new hessian under his arm and, with Bob's help, intended to overhaul the hide, a job that was long overdue.

During these early stages of Operation Osprey coming off watch for six hours seemed like a long holiday. Once more, one very soon learnt the hard way. What with washing and shaving, feeding oneself and washing-up, doing one's share of the camp chores, getting a bit of exercise and sleeping intermittently one's so-called free time slipped by pretty quickly. We were all fresh but it was a long time to the hatch. Goodness alone knows how much tea and coffee we all drank and possibly we might have swallowed even more if the water-fatigue had been a less onerous duty.

Sadly, the two girls had to leave us during the Sunday afternoon. Betty drove off to her home near Aberdeen with a welcome promise to return and help us out at week-ends. Irene had a job with the National Trust for Scotland and George had to drive her into Aviemore so that she could catch a train which landed her back in Edinburgh in the evening. Thus the three pioneers were left on their own until the Conservancy reinforcement arrived. There was, right from the start, a tremendous spirit of *camaraderie*, probably engendered by the very smallness of our numbers. It became a matter of honour to do more than one's fair share of camp chores. This actually resulted in none of us doing more than our fair share but it made it unnecessary for George, who had plenty of problems, to worry about a duty-roster for the Elsan emptying, water-carrying and all those other things that ensured that Operation Osprey was anything but a romantic holiday for those engaged in it.

We got much more than moral support from Iain Grant. The laird was a busy man yet once or twice a week he would come over and take a stint. His efforts were especially valuable because he almost invariably took one of the vital night-watches. He always arrived with a .22 rifle and ammunition. Iain was a capital shot and he always swore that if any blighter climbed the tree during one of his watches he would put a bullet in one of his legs. I am bound to add that I greatly doubt if Iain, even given the opportunity, would have put this threat into practice but the effects on a nocturnal marauder of a shot fired in the general direction of the eyrie might have been extremely discouraging! Right from the beginning, too, we got unexpected and invaluable help from our old friend, Archie Macdonald, who was then the warden of the large and demanding Cairngorms Nature Reserve. It was the height of the nesting season and, being a conscientious man, Archie put in long hours on his job. Yet in his own, limited spare-time he would sometimes drive over about seven o'clock and insist on relieving the duty-watcher until the next change was due at ten. This was an almost miraculous windfall for the man on watch, who was able to stroll to Base Camp, get himself a supper, be tucked up in bed soon after nine and enjoy a full night's sleep. We had our bad times when three or four watchers had to carry the whole burden and better ones when the task was shared between five or six but the one thing we were always short of was sleep—sometimes very short of it indeed.

The weather during that first week was not bad for the time of year. There was little rain although it snowed lightly once or twice; there were some hard night frosts and a fair ration of sunshine. Until the week-end the wind laid pretty low, too, which was very much to our advantage.

Our first watches from the look-out were attractive both because of their novelty and the thrill of an adventure. For all three of us our baptism of fire occurred in broad daylight. The hide was still horribly cramped and the wooden box totally inadequate. If it were placed lengthwise the hard seat was so low that any average-sized individual had to stretch up to be able to see the eyrie through the slit in the sacking, whilst if one set the box on its end, the narrow side resting on the rough, uneven ground, it not only became a rather precarious perch but the seat was now so high that, in order to peer out it became necessary to adopt a sort of hunchbacked attitude, reminiscent of an off-duty osprey resting on its perch. Whichever way you tried to place this cursed box, an early attack of backache could be guaranteed.

During daylight hours, especially so in the mornings, there were the bird-songs and calls around the hide to beguile the time. Little peep-holes, small but more or less circular, had been cut out on both sides of the hide and there was another in the drape at the back through which our entries and exits were made. Occasionally one heard the cheerful call of a crested tit close by and, by peering out through one tiny hole or the other, watch the spritely bird flitting about within a few feet. However, our task was to watch the ospreys. Because of the extreme narrowness of the angle of view there was really little to look at. The incubating bird sat very low in the nest, so that all one could usually see above the rim of the sticks was the head of the bird and, occasionally, the neck as it stretched up to take a look round. If the hen was on the nest the male, if he were not away fishing, would almost certainly be sitting on his favourite perch on a tree which was absolutely invisible from the look-out; even a whole view of an osprey would have been rather more exciting than the distant head of one, usually motionless at that.

Both birds shared in the incubation of the eggs, although it was soon obvious that the female undertook the greater share. If the duty-watcher was lucky he might see two or even perhaps three change-overs during his three-hour spell but although this was a worthwhile spectacle, it only occupied a minute or two, after which he was back again in the humdrum groove of looking at a head and a bit of neck. About once a day the male osprey flew off to the Spey or one of the lochs and brought back a fish. The luckless watcher usually had not the slightest idea that he had left the area and did not at once know when he returned, for he took his prey to his own favourite tree and, with complete lack of gallantry, started feeding himself. Sometimes, after a little experience, one might guess that he had returned with a fish, because the sitting female became more restless, frequently looking about her, occasionally even indulging in high-pitched, peevish mewings. This kind of behaviour always put a strain on the watcher, suggesting that there might be a trespasser about. Eventually the male bird really did provide a break in the monotony by bringing the remains of the fish to the eyrie, so that for a minute or two both birds might be on their feet. Then the female went off with the fish, the male

Keeping a low profile
(Photograph by C. K. Mylne)

settled to brood and things had returned to normal. The chances of seeing this fish ritual were pretty low, however, and it would be truthful to admit that watching the eyrie, even in daylight, was tedious work.

The two night watches, occupying the six hours between ten o'clock in the evening and four the next morning, were quite different. At first I think we all found these watches very strange. If they held many similarities, the two vigils were very different in character. Although the nights got noticeably shorter by the end of the month, in the second week of May the sun sank behind the distant hills around 9.15 p.m. and it did not rise again until after 4.30 a.m. Taking over the watch at ten o'clock, if the sky was clear the light was brilliant in the north-western sky beyond the eyrie: indeed, it was still almost daylight, so that there was no immediate need to resort to field-glasses. If the night were overcast, especially so if the clouds were dark and heavy, the twilight would be deepening even at this hour but the light was strong enough to silhouette the eyrie and the head of the brooding bird clearly enough to satisfy the lone watcher that all was well.

The beginning of this first watch of the evening was enlivened by the songs and calls of the birds. Without taking one's eyes off the eyrie one could listen to shrill squeaks and grumpy snoring calls of woodcock as they passed, mostly unseen, on their curious 'roding' flights, the calls of curlews as well as their songs and the persistent melodies of blackbirds and thrushes. In still weather there were the distant *wee-wee-willock-wee* of the odd lapwing and the squawking cries of black-heads at a small gullery of breeding birds beside a pool, a mile away, close to the little used and narrow road that crosses the Mains of Tulloch. The light would be failing by this time. If it were cloudy it would by now be necessary to make full use of the night-glasses even if the afterglow of day, although it would be shifting disadvantageously round towards the north, was still strong enough for the upper half of the eyrie tree to show up against it as an ill-defined ebony relief.

Each watcher was provided with a whistle of a size and kind that produced a blast similar to those issued to the police. These were always carried about one's person, night or day, awake or asleep, so that if one happened to be wandering round the area of Base Camp or taking a bit of much-needed exercise by strolling round the east end of Loch Garten to see if the male osprey was on his favourite perch, the alarm could be raised if anything happened which suggested that an intruder might be about. By day, had some emergency arisen, these whistles might have been put to good use. There was then likely to be at least one person pottering about at Base Camp and an early experiment showed that, unless there was a good wind blowing in the wrong direction, a watcher in the look-out could hear a whistle on the Mallachie side, even if the blower were five or six hundred yards distant. However, the thickly growing trees round Base Camp muffled the sound of a whistle and greatly reduced its working range. By night, when those up at the camp would be catching up on much-needed sleep, the whistles were almost useless. I say 'almost' because I was always of the opinion that they might have some psychological value if the eyrie were ever raided. When on night-watch I always wore mine hung around my neck on a piece of binder-twine, believing that a few blasts on it might cause an intruder to think that his escape route might be cut off.

Each watcher, at night, also had a pocket-torch. This was essential because it would otherwise have been impossible to follow the rough path safely

Cock osprey feeding on the fish he has caught
(Photograph by C. K. Mylne)

between the firs when walking either to or from the look-out at the one o'clock change-over. It was also useful when in the look-out at night. A larger torch was kept permanently in the hide but a pocket-torch was much easier to handle. As the female brooded continuously from half an hour after sunset until sunrise, night-duty men usually kept their pens in their pockets as once it was getting really dark it was far better not to switch on a torch, even for a few seconds, because it temporarily destroyed night vision.

If a daylight watch in the hide sometimes seemed tediously prolonged, these night stints often seemed endless. Once the light had failed it was essential to use the night-glasses almost continuously. By then the eyrie was nothing more than a blurred splodge. After some minutes of sustained watching through binoculars I used to find that the black blob changed its outline, rather like some mirage. The female sat pretty tight throughout the night and when, in near darkness, she occasionally rose and stood for a few seconds in the nest before turning round and resettling, it was only because the watcher knew that

Alighting on the eyrie, fish in talons
(Photograph by Hans and Judy Beste/Ardea, London)

she did this sort of thing as a matter of habit which enabled him to convince himself that the wobbling outline of the flat top of the eyrie was probably real enough and not a figment of his imagination.

The last half of that first stint of the night was never easy going. It was cheerless, dark and often very cold. Under clear, windless skies, frost would settle over the marsh even before midnight. Feet and fingers became numb. There was nothing to be done about one's feet but occasionally, if all seemed quiet and serene, one could drop the night-glasses, stuff one's aching fingers under one's armpits and suffer the agony of circulation returning whilst one carried on with eyes skinned and ears pricked.

In the darkness the silence was often remarkably impressive. In the still weather it sat on one with a claustrophobic intensity. After nightfall the birds at the distant gullery, apart from an occasional brief eruption, remained quiet until first light. The deep hush might be interrupted by the faraway bleatings of a sheep, the tremulous hoot of a distant tawny owl or some other familiar, friendly sound. There were other sounds that only added to the anxieties of the watcher. If the faint call of a curlew was pleasant enough, if one rose crying and flying around within a few hundred yards of the eyrie tree one immediately suspected the possibility of a stranger on the prowl—and rightly so. There were plenty of foxes and roe-deer in the neighbourhood. Both animals are active at night. There was one occasion when a presumed roebuck, galloping quickly over a bit of firm, dry ground to the rear of the look-out, made me think, however momentarily, that I was about to be ambushed by a posse of mounted egg-collectors. The crack of even a small twig would often cut the stillness with the sharpness of a knife. If the sound came from the vicinity of the eyrie tree the luckless watcher, as blind as a bat insofar as any movements at ground level were concerned, had to listen intently, striving all the time to make out at least something of the nebulous, shadowy nest to see if the sitting bird became uneasy enough to stand up and, perhaps, fly off into the inky darkness. We did not even know, of course, whether the ospreys would react to an intruder by night in the same violent way as we had seen and heard them do by day. Lacking experience, it was inevitable that, during those lonely vigils, we largely worked by guess and by God.

After it was quite dark the time always dragged. If there was much to keep the watcher on the *qui vive*, there was nothing to look at. During daylight one could at least glance hopefully at one's watch from time to time but at night (unless, of course, one had a watch with a luminous dial, which I had not) this necessitated switching on a torch, an operation always to be avoided if possible. Fortunately I have a fair working knowledge of astronomy and on clear nights I could watch the pair of bright stars in Gemini, Castor and Pollux, as they began to decline towards their setting in the north-west; they provided an approximate indication of the passing of time. On still nights the trains on the Highland railway through Speyside from Perth to Inverness were mostly audible between Newtonmore and Carr Bridge. There was a southbound train from Inverness that reached Aviemore around 12.45 a.m. and, with luck, one could pick up the friendly clattering of this sleeper when it trundled through Carr Bridge. It was music on the ears: in half an hour or so the vigil would be over, which signified much more than merely the end of a period of strain and discomfort. It meant a chance to stretch cramped limbs and warm arms and legs; to brew up a pot of hot tea in the snug, well-lit comfort of the caravan and finally to discard boots, jacket and trousers and forget everything in sound sleep.

Unless there was a strong wind one heard the footsteps of the relief quite a while before he arrived. I never finally made up my mind, after ample experience of both, which of the two night watches was the lesser of two evils. Certainly the second watch involved one being plunged in at the deep end at the outset. Thus there was the psychological advantage of knowing that things would improve in due time, at least to the extent that one would finish the stint in daylight. On the other hand this watch was the colder of the two. I soon discovered that another friendly train was well worth listening out for, because it heralded the end of the worst of the darkness. It was a northbound train this time, scheduled to make its exit from the Pass of Drumochter around Dalwhinnie and to clatter down into Strathspey a little before two o'clock. On any clear day from Loch Mallachie there is an uninterrupted view right up the Spey valley for a score of miles or more. With high hills on either side the glen was something of a funnel, carrying loud sounds over long distances, especially in the stillness of the night. Until the train was approaching Newtonmore station it could not be heard at all because of intervening mountains. The distant clippety-cloppety rattle struck suddenly on the ears with all the welcome warmth of some far-off choir of angels. I came to love the sound of that train more than any other one associated with Operation Osprey. Soon after its mellow roar became audible it subsided and finally ceased as the train stopped for a few minutes at Newtonmore. Then the glad noise was renewed as it rolled on to its next stop at Kingussie. After another short pause it trundled on down the long stretch of line before grinding to a halt in Aviemore. If my memory does not play me false, the time was about 2.30 a.m. and, unless it was overcast, the first glimmer of dawn was beginning to puncture the darkness.

If those trains could be regarded as good allies, cars passing in the night, even if most were harmless enough, were always regarded as hostile. During the day there was a modest volume of traffic along the road skirting the eastern shore of Loch Garten but only the odd vehicle used the lonely route across the Mains of Tulloch. After dusk there was little on the move and practically none at all between midnight and breakfast time. In quiet or reasonably quiet weather it was usually possible, from the look-out, to catch the sound of a car or lorry for a few seconds as it passed the far end of Loch Garten, almost a mile away. In the peace of the night the noise seemed much louder than it really was. If at any time after sunset a watcher pricked up his ears to the sound of any vehicle, once it was growing dark he listened very intently, waiting to see if the car halted or passed right through. Sometimes a car could be heard grinding up the Tulloch road at the back of the hide. If it stopped one might at least suspect that somebody was undertaking a reconnaissance of the upper end of the marsh, if not worse.

In any raid on the eggs of any rare bird, the attacker always has the advantage of being able to choose his own time. George and I were always convinced that any egg-collector would make his final assault on the citadel sometime between last light and first light. Bob Dawkins, somewhat to our astonishment, held stubbornly to the opinion that any such attempt would be made either in daylight or strong twilight. If a collector were to try to lift the eggs I always hoped that, barring a thick, early morning mist, it would be made in daylight. Even if the attacker was able to reach the base of the eyrie tree without unduly disturbing the ospreys and probably giving himself away thereby, which I considered improbable, he would certainly be spotted almost as soon as he began to scale the tree. By comparison with conditions of near-darkness it would be easier for the raider to climb to the eyrie and pouch the eggs but, even if he reached the ground before being intercepted, his chances of making a successful escape in broad daylight, in my belief, would have been greatly reduced.

Right from the start George was worried about the two night shifts, with one watcher working entirely on his own. It was not long before he came up with the answer to this urgent problem.

The first warden from the Nature Conservancy, complete with a very useful land-rover, arrived on schedule. During the course of the ensuing weeks we enjoyed the splendid help, in turn, of three wardens from the Conservancy: Jimmy Polson, Langley Roberts and my friend, Louis Stewart. It would be difficult to overrate their contribution to Operation Osprey. Jimmy was quiet

A female osprey with the remains of a fish
(Photograph by C. K. Mylne)

and reserved but very efficient; Langley as conscientious as they come, was one of the most cheerful pseudo-grumblers I have ever met; 'Big Louis' was a tower of strength, both literally and metaphorically. Not one of them, although they made many helpful suggestions, ever bothered to question the broad strategy of the operation; all of them worked with almost tireless energy and enthusiasm and, off-duty, they added their quota to what little fun could be extracted from our restricted lives of watches, chores and, whenever possible, a few hours blessed, blessed sleep, with all its oblivion and freedom from care. I reckon that the only time when any of us were not worried as to whether or not the eyrie would be attacked in the next twenty-four hours was when they were unconscious.

As soon as Jimmy Polson arrived George whistled off down to Edinburgh. He was only away for one night, Jimmy taking his place in our rota. George's object was to hire and bring back a number of tents, so that the caravan could be used solely for culinary and recreational purposes, and to rustle up 'volunteers' to cover some of the less demanding daylight watches. I anticipated his return on the following evening with unashamed delight. For the first time for three days, with a rota of four watchers instead of three, we should have a chance to get at least five or six hours of uninterrupted sleep in every twenty-four. I appreciated that, with four persons each doing three-hour stints at the look-out, if strict rotation was adhered to, we should always be doing the same periods of duty. In what spare time I had I used paper and pencil in various ingenious attempts to get round this problem only to discover to my chagrin, immediately on George's return, that all my precious time had been wasted.

George arrived back loaded with a number of small, one-man tents, complete with poles, guys and pegs; safari-type camp-beds (what a luxury!) and a good supply of those warm but rough blankets that cause feet and chin to itch on the slightest provocation. He also brought the good news that, within a couple of days, two volunteers would arrive and stay for a week or ten days, thus taking care of most of the watches between seven o'clock in the morning and seven in the evening. All this was welcome news but we really pricked up our ears when he told us that he had solved the vexed problem of the lonely night vigils.

His plan was simple but damnably good. A tent would be erected a few yards behind the look-out in a position completely screened from the ospreys on the eyrie. This tent would be equipped with a safari-bed, a blanket or two and a pillow, as well as a big torch. Watchers who were relieved at 10.0 p.m., 1.0 a.m. and 4.0 a.m., instead of returning at once to Base Camp as hitherto, would retire to this tent for the next three hours. They would not be permitted even to remove their boots but at least they could lie down at full-length, easing their cramped limbs, as well as covering themselves with a blanket or two to keep out the cold. George intended to beg some binder-twine from Iain Grant (an easy target for any beggars in the cause of the ospreys, anyway). A length of this binder-twine would run, without any slackness, between the look-out and the tent in the rear. A watcher retiring to this tent would, as soon as he settled down in his rough-and-ready bunk, put his end of the twine, which would have a well-secured loop in it, round his right arm, whilst the duty-watcher at the other end of the line would stuff it into the right-hand pocket of his jacket, so that he knew just where to grab hold of it instead of groping around in the dark or fumbling for a torch in order to find it.

This alarm system was simple, silent and highly effective. A really strong

George Waterston in the hide erected at Loch Garten in 1958
(Photograph by Tom Weir)

yank on the look-out end of the line went some considerable way towards dislocating the arm of the body at the other end. It was then only a matter of seconds for the dozing party to slip his arm out of the loop and roll out on to his feet. Torch in hand, he could be alongside the look-out within twenty or thirty seconds, booted and ready for action.

The following day our rather meagre ration of sleep was reduced even further. Apart from the man on watch, once the usual camp chores were done everybody was involved in a feverish burst of activity. One tent and the necessary equipment were humped down to a strip of fairly flat ground behind the look-out. The tent was pitched with the minimum of fuss and noise. The ground was pretty soft below the surface and there was no necessity to drive the wooden pegs in with a mallet. Then the safari-bed, with pillow and bolster on top of the pile, was set up in readiness for the first occupant at ten o'clock that evening. It was going to be a long time before those blankets were again to be folded up so neatly!

George Waterston and our primitive alarm system, asleep in a nearby tent
(Photograph by Tom Weir)

In the afternoon George had everybody at it again, pitching the tents at Base Camp. I recollect that about six tents were pitched altogether, each as far from its neighbour as possible in order that, given due care, anybody getting up for duty would be unlikely to wake a sleeping neighbour. When the work was done the clearing, dotted with small white tents and with the caravan and George's Dormobile dominating the scene, looked something like a real settlement. George intended to continue to use his vehicle to enjoy what sleep he could get. Bob and Jimmy and I had a tent apiece. Two tents would be available for the first two 'volunteers' who were due to arrive soon, leaving one spare. George, as CO, not only directed his troops but took his share of the hard labour. If we lost a bit of sleep the exercise did us all a lot of good. It was splendid to have the caravan as a community centre, so that one no longer had to tiptoe about like a verger in his temple lest one should wake a sleeper. All this, coupled with the knowledge that on future night stints at the look-out we should have a rear-guard as a back-up in any emergency, was a great boost to morale.

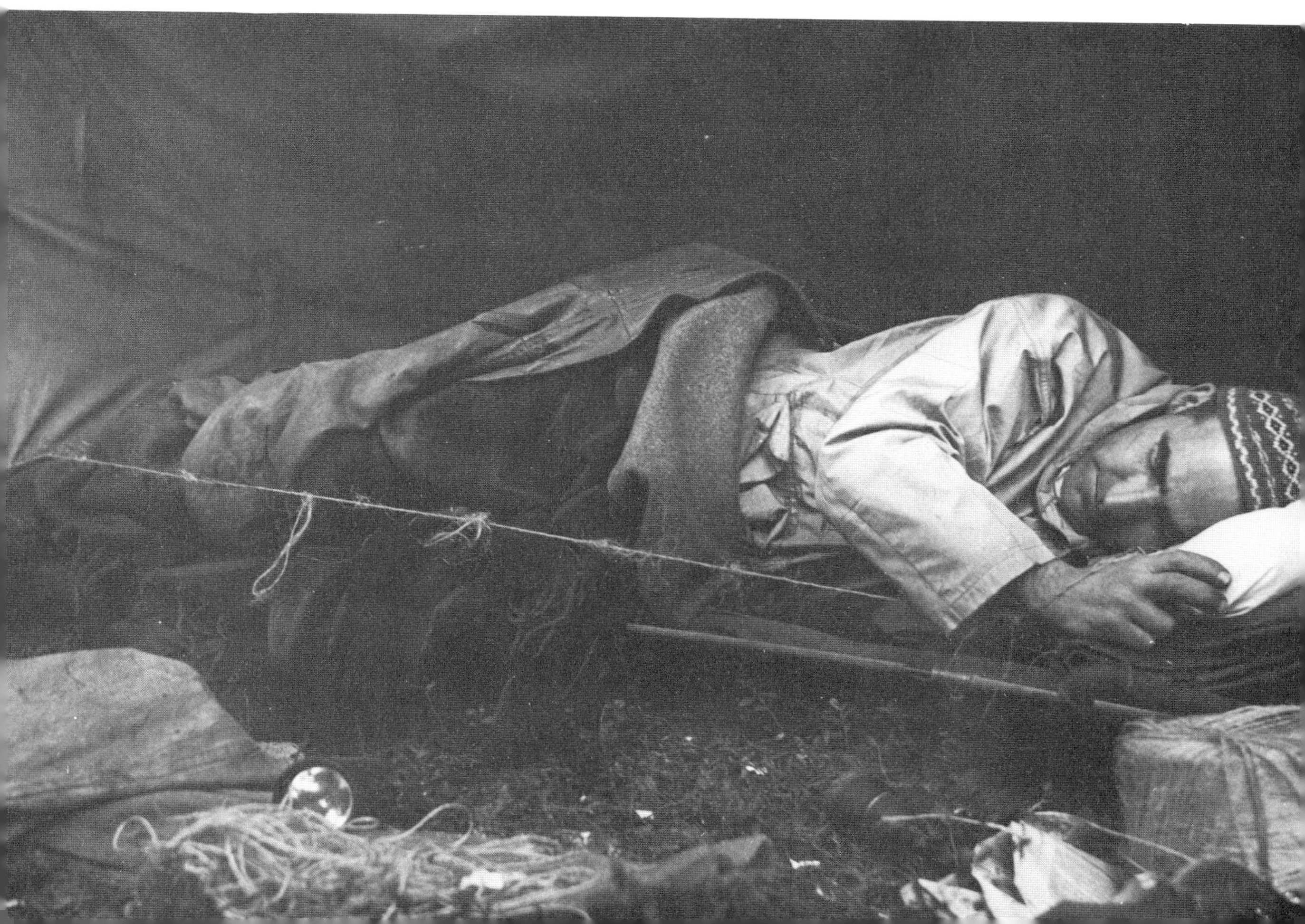

It was about this time that Archie Macdonald turned up one evening at the look-out when I was on watch and offered to relieve me for an hour or two. I gladly surrendered my place in the hide, tired of the hardness of the confounded wooden box, but it was a quiet, fine evening and Archie was always good company. I settled down immediately behind the look-out and we chatted away in low tones. Although he was genuinely thrilled to bits about the whole business, Archie was not the first watcher to express some disappointment over the general lack of activity at the eyrie. We both agreed that it would probably be much more entertaining when there were young chicks in the nest.

Archie a big, thick-set individual, soon found the constricting hide unbearable, suggesting that if more hessian were available it could easily be improved. As I knew that the remainder of the roll of sacking was up in Base Camp I tripped light-heartedly up the path to fetch it, leaving Archie in charge of the ospreys.

Archie was large enough physically to appear clumsy. He also had big hands, which do not always go with good craftsmanship. I retired and lay down some distance to the rear of the hide where I could keep an eye both on the eyrie and Archie. The latter, as a spectacle, was by far the more interesting. He worked on that hide so quietly that the brooding bird, although it must have been able to see some movement, displayed little or no concern. In half an hour or so, with the minimum of fuss and maximum of efficiency, Archie Macdonald transformed that look-out almost beyond belief. Its cubic capacity was just about doubled, for one thing, and the whole structure was firmer, the roof no longer sagging badly in the middle. Within twenty-four hours Iain Grant paid us one of his visits. Maybe the duty-watcher complained about the hardness of his seat but, anyway, Iain quickly assessed the potential of the new, roomier version of the hide. He drove off in his land-rover and was soon back with an ancient but comfortable armchair, complete with a varied supply of old cushions so that the duty-watcher could sit at the right height to see the eyrie tree through the front slit.

This was only the first part of the chain reaction triggered off by Archie. On my suggestion we invested a few shillings in a square yard of rubber sheeting. Spread over the roof and securely fastened with safety-pins this kept most of the rain out on wet days. It was also decided to improve the watcher's view of the eyrie and its immediate vicinity by enlarging the frontal slit. The ospreys appeared to have accepted our minimal amount of disturbance without demur but, playing safe, the extension to the front slit was, at first, fastened up with more safety-pins, so that it could be lowered again if necessary. It never was

Two very young chicks in their eyrie
(Photograph by K. Fink/Ardea, London)

necessary. Ever thoughtful of his troops, George produced two thermos flasks, one for each of the two night-duty men. This enabled the chap who was relieved at 1.0 a.m. to sit on his bunk in the tent behind the look-out and swallow two or three cupfuls of warming 'Nescafé' before stretching out, whilst his colleague who had taken over waited until it was getting really light, which might be any time between three and four o'clock, before broaching his flask with its equally invigorating effect. A couple of blankets were also draped over the new chair in the hide. On frosty nights a watcher no longer suffered that numbness which made it necessary, every now and then, to feel for boots in order to reassure himself that they were still attached to a pair of seemingly dead feet. Those of us in the small band who pioneered the osprey watches in 1958 are unlikely to forget our debts to Archie Macdonald and Iain Grant.

It was a curious existence. One day succeeded another with a degree of monotony which gave birth to one of my few original sayings: 'Today is the Yesterday of Tomorrow'. The routine was restrictive and largely humdrum.

As far as I can recall there was seldom, if ever, any alcohol on the camp. We drank endless cups of tea and coffee, mixed with soft drinks such as orangeade and barley water. We fed pretty well in a simple, almost primitive way. Apart from the lack of adequate equipment to prepare anything elaborate, we had no time to be fussy. We lived largely out of tins but we also had fresh meat, potatoes and carrots so that we could enjoy warming stews for supper. These stews were simmered in an enormous saucepan placed on one of the calor-gas burners. This saucepan was only cleaned out once or twice a week, the eternal stews kept going simply by adding to what was left from the day before. Later on in May H. E. (Bert) Axell, who was just about to take over as warden of the Minsmere bird reserve of the RSPB, came up to join the team. I vividly recall one evening when the stew-pot was discovered empty and none of us had thought about any replenishments. Bert Axell made light of this *contretemps*. Without bothering to seek any advice, he opened a number of tins of canned beans, corned beef and, finally, a large tin of peaches. Next he chucked in a tin of curry powder, stirred up the well-filled saucepan for a few minutes and then, as it began to simmer, retired to the other end of the caravan to read the tattered remains of yesterday's newspaper, shrugging off such remarks as 'Why the peaches?' or 'How do you know we all like curry?' with all the easy non-chalance of the professional chef who knows what's best for his clients. The ensuing meal was filling enough but Bert had rather overdone the curry. We ate in silence, wiping away our tears with handkerchiefs that were probably a bit on the grubby side. So we had our bits of fun but they were few and far between.

On weekday mornings there was the duty-run to Boat-of-Garten to fetch supplies. This was a chance for some to see a bit of civilization and to knock back a quick pint of ale at the hotel. Most of us tried to snatch an hour sometime during the day to get away from the camp where one could see little except tight-knit conifers and a patch of sky. The exercise was beneficial and it was good to have a change of scene, enjoying one's own thoughts without fear of interruption. Living more or less on top of one another it was inevitable that, however rarely, tempers could become frayed but we had too much respect for one another for these absurd tiffs to last more than a few minutes. Psychologically they may have done some good in relieving the monotony and the tension of the job.

If that impertinent egg-collector had not reached the eyrie tree on May 10 and had the cheek to climb up and take a brief look in the nest we should never have known that the female osprey had laid the first egg of her clutch earlier that morning. It is just possible that she might have laid that first egg on the previous day because the eggs of a clutch are usually produced at intervals of forty-eight hours but the behaviour of the birds suggested otherwise to our admittedly inexperienced eyes. May 10 was therefore the date on which we reckoned incubation had begun: the hen certainly and the cock probably sat low in the nest for periods of that day and the female settled to brood long before dusk. It was presumed that incubation would last for 35 days before the first chick could be expected to hatch, which fixed D-Day for June 14. We were probably over-optimistic to the extent of two or three days but it made no matter.

I suppose it was George who devised a simple board on which were written, in serial style, all the numbers from 1–34 inclusive. It might have been better if the 35th square had carried the heartening sign of D-Day and the days had been numbered backwards, in which case we should have begun with D-Day minus 34, enjoying all the psychological advantage of being in the twenties before our long-sustained effort had really begun to test our stamina and, at times, our fortitude. However, this was a small point; the idea of the marker-board was a good one. George produced a large blue pencil that hung on a piece of string by the board and this was used to cross off, always boldly, each day as it passed. It came to be tacitly regarded as the privilege of the man going on duty at one o'clock in the morning to keep this board up to date. It was always a great moment: one day more and one day less. At that hour of the night most Britons would be fast asleep, utterly oblivious of our efforts to safeguard a pair of breeding ospreys in this wild and lonely neck of the Highlands. It might still be a long way off but the time would come when the chicks would be safely hatched and all the world could share in our moment of triumph. It was at least an encouraging thought!

The routine, as I have stressed, was both demanding and monotonous, yet I remember I was sorry when, at the end of the first week, I felt bound to return to London to spend a few days in all the comfort of an office chair. I planned to work very hard and bring everything up to date, so that I could return on the following week-end. There would even then be three weeks to go before we could expect the eggs to hatch and I knew very well, come what may, once I returned I would see it out to the finish.

I recollect that a spell of generally pleasant weather broke on the day of my departure. I had booked a sleeper on the train to Edinburgh that left Aviemore some time after midnight. Iain Grant had come over to do a spell of watching in the evening and after dark he drove me into Aviemore in his land-rover.

There was a wild south-westerly in full blow and a waxing moon peeping shyly through odd gaps in the scudding clouds. When we drove past the eastern fringe of Loch Garten the wavelets, lashed by the storm, were splashing on the shore. I felt sorry for the duty-men, even though it was relatively warm. They would be able to hear nothing except the howling of the wind and if the clouds thickened the moon had not waxed enough to afford any worthwhile light. My sympathy may have been wasted because this wild night would have been far from suitable for any egg-collector to contemplate a raid on the eyrie.

On my return to Speyside it was easy to drop back into the old routine. George had to pay one or two brief visits to Edinburgh and there were hard times when we were reduced to four and occasionally three watchers. We had a pleasant windfall when a splendid chap from Cornwall, F. J. Willcocks, landed up in the neighbourhood and, hearing about the ospreys, came along and offered his services for an indefinite period. Willcocks must have been almost seventy, if not older, at that time but he was a tower of strength, ever willing to take on an extra watch at any time between seven in the morning and ten in the evening. I remember that he was desperately keen to be allowed to do a night watch but, bearing in mind his age, I agreed with George's decision that this could not be allowed.

Betty Garden and Irene Waterston often came at week-ends and then we were all in clover, enjoying wonderful meals and being excused from washing-up afterwards. Betty presented us with a very business-like 'cosh' and this was hung up on a handy hook in the look-out. We often discussed exactly what we might do if we caught an egg-collector *in flagranti delicto*. It was generally agreed that the best plan was to strip him to the buff, inform him that we would take all his clothing to the nearest police station and then turn him loose. If this sounds like rough justice it was a heartwarming thought for any of us on duty.

Whilst May still had three or four days to run we reckoned that we were half way through our task. It was always possible, of course, that some unforeseeable disaster might overtake the ospreys after the chicks had hatched out. There was, however, never any intention of abandoning our watches when that glad time came. For a week or ten days afterwards George intimated that he

Meal-time at the eyrie
(Photograph by Joe Van Wormer/Bruce Coleman Limited)

hoped to continue the round-the-clock watches, if only because a marauding egg-collector might not know that the nest no longer contained eggs. After that it should not be necessary to maintain night watches at all. The object would then be to keep the eyrie free from disturbances from innocent walkers and other tourists and as such folk were unlikely to be around much before breakfast-time or after dusk, it would only be necessary to man the look-out from about seven or eight o'clock in the morning until ten or eleven in the evening.

Incubation had been going on for three weeks and it was only a fortnight to D-Day. We could not, of course, be sure of the exact date but June 14 had become generally accepted. I think we also took heart from a belief that the longer the eggs were incubated the less desirable they might seem as a prize for an egg-collector. The fresher the eggs the better, yet we all knew that any competent collector could handle a hard-set clutch. And we never forgot that a clutch of osprey eggs taken in the Highlands of Scotland was probably the most attractive bait that had been dangled in front of collectors in years. We could not afford to relax until we were certain that the eyrie contained small chicks.

The nights shortened very noticeably during the last three weeks of May. On fine evenings the sun did not sink behind the distant Monadhliaths until nearly ten o'clock and even an hour later the twilight was still so strong that watching from the look-out was almost as easy as in full daylight. Even at midnight (British Summer Time, which means that this was, in fact, an hour before real midnight) the eyrie remained clearly silhouetted against a bright, clear sky. Half an hour later things became more difficult, not only because the light had faded but because the afterglow of the sunset had shifted round into the north, The next hour-and-a-half demanded the most exacting concentration, especially so now that the full moon had waned to a crescent and was no longer of any use to us. But if the sky was free from cloud the dim light of early dawn began to penetrate the marsh around two o'clock. On overcast nights the light faded earlier and dawn broke later, almost doubling the hours of darkness.

George Kerr and Jimmy Campbell were two stalwart volunteers who kept returning for more punishment. No longer young except in heart they were indefatigable and having been friends for many years often went on watch together. Both were remarkable characters: George dour and reliable; Jimmy, equally reliable, bubbling over with fun and laughter and making light of his troubles. This unforgettable pair did a lot to strengthen the morale of their comrades.

CHAPTER NINE

A Clutch for the Taking

June 2, 1958, was one of those indifferent days which not infrequently occur early in that month. There was little wind but there was also little sun and it remained cool for the time of year. A layer of heavy stratus settled over Speyside late in the afternoon, suggesting rain might be on the way. Bert Axell and I were on the duty-roster for the two night watches. Bert was on at ten o'clock and I was due to relieve him three hours later.

I enjoyed my dinner with the others in the caravan about eight o'clock, refreshed by a spell of sleep in the late afternoon. Then, ever in need of exercise, I went off for a stroll, spending a few minutes by the eastern shore of Loch Garten. After lighting a pipe, I ambled up the track to Loch Mallachie. For any person, like myself, who hankers after wild places, the setting of this small loch takes a bit of beating. On this grey, windless evening, it was superb. The water was like a mirror and, bird songs and calls apart, it was enchantingly peaceful. I lay down full-length in the heather and finished smoking my pipe. By then it was ten o'clock and although the invisible sun would only just have set, the light was already beginning to wane. I was reluctant to move, however, and sat on in this peaceful solitude until the dusk had really gathered and the last of the thrushes had fallen silent. Feeling chilly, I retraced my steps at a brisk pace but by the time I turned off the road on to the track that led down through the thick-set conifers to the clearing it seemed dark already. It was good to see the lights of the caravan winking through the trees but when I reached it about eleven o'clock everybody had gone to bed.

It was pleasantly warm in the caravan and I settled down to amuse myself

Hen osprey taking off nest
(Photograph by C. K. Mylne)

for an hour or so in the routine way, taking a look at the latest newspaper and the odd, dog-eared magazine, keeping a wary eye on the time. It was so quiet and windless that one could have heard a spider running across the floor. The odd mosquito buzzed around irritatingly. The chart on the wall was beginning to look uncommonly cheerful, with all the numbers up to and including 23 already crossed off and in a few minutes it would be the end of the twenty-fourth. Only eleven days to go until D-Day which meant, with any luck, not more than perhaps half-a-dozen night-watches as far as I was concerned—and most of them were likely to be a good deal less dark than this one. A little mental arithmetic was enough to satisfy me that our job was two-thirds done. I wondered whether George would sanction a bit of a 'booze-up' to celebrate the hatching of the osprey eggs after so many years of frustration and disappointment.

Midnight came and the time to brew up tea. I also made myself a bully-beef butty, wrapping it up carefully in the most ancient newspaper I could find and stuffing it in the pocket of my jacket as an insurance against any hunger pangs I might suffer when I came off watch and retired to the rear tent at four o'clock. I put a fair measure of coffee extract into my thermos-flask and filled it with hot water. I like my coffee black and it would help to wash the butty down in due time. George was due to relieve me at four o'clock and George was never late. As a matter of fact nobody was ever late on watch and it was a point of honour, at night, to be a few minutes early.

It was half-past twelve and almost time to set out. I swilled the tea-leaves round the pot and tossed them out into the gloom. Then I tidied the tables, put on my jacket, checked that I had all the essentials with me, switched on my torch and turned off the caravan lighting. I was blissfully unaware of the somewhat startling fact that, at that moment, a man was lying-up under cover pretty close to that stunted pine tree which held the ospreys' nest and all our hopes. With the aid of the torch I gave myself the ultimate pleasure of scoring off the figure 24 on the chart with the blue pencil, let myself out of the caravan, slipped on the first step and fell head-over-heels on to the mercifully softish ground. I was not hurt and if I swore I hope I did so very quietly, for two or three weary souls were asleep within earshot. The torch was undamaged and, thank goodness, so was the flask of coffee.

It was a very still night without a breath of wind and it seemed as black as pitch among the firs as I threaded my lonely way down the familiar and, by now, well-trodden track. On the final approach to the look-out post the trees suddenly thinned considerably but, for once, it seemed as dark there as in the thickest of the forest.

Slightly alarmed by the intrusion
(Photograph by C. K. Mylne)

I first went to the rear tent to announce my arrival to the stand-by, so that he could nip away to the camp. Lucky devil, I thought to myself, as I went forward to relieve Bert Axell. Bert seldom complained but, on this night, he laid a curse on the depth of the darkness. However, he told me that his watch had been very quiet and was able to confirm that the female was on the nest even if it was too dark to see the top of her head above the rim of the extremely dim silhouette of the eyrie. He vacated the chair and plodded back to the tent behind, probably as thankful as I knew I should be in three hours time.

It was, in fact, a mild night by Speyside standards in early June. I went through the familiar routine, checking that the big torch was by my feet and feeling for Betty Garden's comforting 'cosh' which, as usual, was dangling from its hook. Then I peered out through the night-glasses and giving a tug at the binder-twine, got the reassuring tug in response which confirmed that Bert had secured it round his right arm. I tucked the end of it into my right-hand pocket with a feeling of satisfaction.

Just after 1 a.m. I suddenly became aware of a very small but very curious noise. It was a steady, muffled rustling the like of which I had never heard before. I still remember that my spine tingled and my right hand went instinctively into my pocket to get a grip on the binder-twine whilst I continued to hold my night-glasses with the other, but if this was a raid I reckoned it must be an army of egg-collectors on the move because the soft, prickly humming seemed to come from all directions. It was several seconds before I realized that it was raining. . . .

The shower was a light one (about the only thing that was light in that infernal canopy of darkness) and the pattering of raindrops ceased within four or five minutes. The stillness was broken by a more familiar and more welcome sound: the night train for Inverness had already puffed out of Newtonmore, barely audible so far off, and was now clattering down towards Aviemore. By the time it reached Aviemore the darkness would surely be breaking up at last. Funny how the rattling of the train, increasing in volume as it slowly got closer, would suddenly cease completely as it passed through a cutting, to return again in a kind of wave as it re-emerged.

The rain stopped about half-past one and it had gone very quiet again. Yet it remained as dark as ever and my eyes were starting to bulge with the sustained effort of peering at the vague blob of the eyrie. Instantaneously something extraordinary happened. Even as I watched, the top half of the eyrie suddenly broke away from the rest of the structure and vanished. It took a second or two for the reality to register in a tired brain; the sitting bird had flown off, This sort of thing had happened before during night-watches but never, at least so far as I was concerned, when it was pitch dark. It threw me into a high degree of alertness. I had one hand back on the binder-twine. I listened intently for any high-pitched alarm cries from the osprey but there were none. I lowered my night-glasses slowly down the tree below the eyrie. I was able to satisfy myself that nobody was in the upper half of the Scots pine: below that all was still wrapped in darkness. Then, as suddenly as it had parted from the eyrie, the black blob returned to it. The osprey had come back and insofar as it was possible to discern anything, she seemed to settle down to incubate. I concluded that the bird had indulged in a brief flight to exercise cramped limbs. Sitting in that look-out hide for hour after hour one soon learnt to have considerable respect for the incubating bird; on night-shifts, at any rate during darkness and deep twilight, the duty-watcher could not even afford himself the luxury of spending a penny!

Some time soon after two o'clock, it began to get light. Soon I could see the outline of the head of the osprey above the dark rim of the huge nest. Twice she stretched up her neck and bobbed her head as she looked around but she did not appear to be alarmed, settling down again after a few seconds.

Suddenly, unexpectedly, the sitting osprey rose from the nest, screaming with alarm. This was a 'red alert'. I lowered my glasses down the tree and saw that the lowest of the visible branches was shaking and waving violently. As it was windless the penny dropped at once. I let my binoculars fall to the ground, heaved myself out of the chair, pulled the alarm cord to rouse Bert Axell in the rear tent, seized the cosh and shot out of the back of the hide.

As Bert emerged from the tent I had time to shout to him that there was a chap up the tree before I ran on to the marsh. The twilight was still deepish, the going on the marsh both rough and soggy. The wetness sucked at my heavy boots and the rough tussocks impeded progress. I had enough breath left to blow my whistle and shout 'Come on, chaps, we've got him now' as I looked up at the tree and saw, with horror, a shadowy figure at the very top. In looking up I measured my length by tripping over one of the many tussocks and buried my face in a puddle of cold, peaty water. By the time I was on my feet again Bert was alongside.

We ploughed on at our best speed but we must have been at least thirty or forty yards short of the tree when the raider dropped out of it and ran off into the thick birch cover between the eyrie and Loch Garten.

One thing was certain: the raider had had remarkably little time at the eyrie itself. Running across that marsh one only saw things by halves but I have no doubt that we took the intruder by surprise. I was under a strong impression that, in his haste, he dropped out of the tree when he was still eight or ten feet above ground. He was certainly under pressure because, given a few more seconds, we should have ambushed him 'good and proper'. Standing below the tree, breathing rather heavily in the pearly morning light and with both ospreys wheeling around and screaming their hearts out it was obvious that, temporarily anyway, the raider had made his escape. We both went off into the birch scrub, occasionally stopping to listen but either the stranger had managed to get clear of the area or, more likely, was lying up in some thick cover until the commotion died down.

Not wishing to leave the nest unguarded I wandered back to the eyrie tree whilst Bert continued to hunt around. I was prepared to give him two or three minutes but not more. The old birds were still circling above the marsh, calling in their distress. Although there was no frost it was chilly and, if there were any eggs left in the eyrie it was important to get off the ground as soon as possible in order that the female could return to incubate them before they became too cold.

Standing by the tree I spotted a curious, whitish patch in the thickish ground growth below the eyrie. It was a smashed osprey's egg containing a well-developed embryo. It seemed that, in making his escape, the marauder had dropped and smashed at least one of the osprey eggs. As I handled that

An angry, young osprey chick
(Photograph by Pekka Helo/Bruce Coleman Limited)

particular end to all our hopes I can still recall that I did not feel vindictive. It was the end of a long and tiring night in which I had striven my utmost and still failed. I just felt rather numb and, now that the adrenalin had ceased to flow, rather weary too.

Bert Axell came back, snorting with frustration. Curiously enough he had never caught sight of the raider either up the tree or dropping down to his freedom. I showed him the smashed egg to prove my point. I wanted to get off the marsh and give the birds a chance but it was first necessary to ascertain what remained in the nest. Bert, as strong as a horse, clambered up the tree in the grey morning light with the agility of a monkey. 'It's okay,' he called down: 'There are still two eggs in the nest.' I know that I cried 'Thank God' and I doubt if I ever did so with more sincerity.

We walked back to the look-out post. We reckoned that the osprey must have laid a clutch of three eggs. The raider, caught by surprise, presumably dropped the one I held in my hand, leaving the two. I think we counted ourselves lucky. Provided the female returned to brood her remaining two eggs without undue delay, Operation Osprey could still be a success, even if one chick had been lost.

Only a few minutes had elapsed since the raider had fled the field. There was still a chance that he might yet be brought to book. I left Bert Axell at the look-out and set off for Base Camp to give the alarm, half running and half trotting up the rising track. I have no exact record of the time but it must have been after three o'clock and getting really light when I beat a tattoo on the back of George Waterston's vehicle. He was asleep and when he opened up he had an interrogative look in his glazed eyes, as if asking what in the name of blazes I thought I was doing rousing him so roughly at this unearthly hour.

Panting for breath, I managed to gasp out: 'There's been a raid.' 'You're joking,' was all he said. In my long life I have never experienced a more bathetic moment. It took me only a few seconds to convince him that I was in earnest and then he was galvanized into action. Within two minutes he had the other three or four sleepers in the camp not only awake but dressing at best speed. Within five minutes he was roaring off in his Dormobile, closely followed by Louis Stewart in the Nature Conservancy land-rover, both intent upon combing all the approach roads to Loch Garten. The other spare watchers were given instructions to search the cover in and around the loch, taking care not to disturb the ospreys. I plodded down the track to rejoin Bert Axell, who was happy to report that the female was back on the eyrie.

I told Bert what George was doing and then dispatched him to Base Camp to get himself breakfast and a bit of well-earned sleep. He had been on duty since ten o'clock and must have been tired out even if he did not show it. As the duty-watcher who should have come on at four o'clock was George himself, I settled in the look-out to await events. It was full daylight now and the task was easy enough. It was not long before I was able to appreciate that the disturbance at the end of the night had upset the birds. The female, whilst sitting her eggs, was constantly bobbing up and down and the male often flying around. But I felt confident that they would settle down in time. It was reassuring to know that two eggs still remained in the nest. Even if only one hatched then, provided the chick was safely reared to maturity, all the frustrations of previous years would be forgotten, our efforts would be rewarded and we could anticipate the next season with high hopes. One way and another, I reckoned we had not come out of the ordeal too badly.

When George arrived at the look-out to take over what remained of his watch I was able to report 'all quiet' although the female had not really yet settled to incubate as quietly as she had done before the disturbance. I went back to camp to enjoy a much-needed wash and shave, followed by a good breakfast which I ate on my own because all the others except Bert Axell, who had gone to his bed, were scouring the highways and byways. George had failed to find any car parked in the vicinity but the villain might well have been lying up in cover, waiting for the brou-ha-ha to die down.

We had no clue as to the identity of the raider. He had got up the tree and subsequently dropped down and scampered off with the nimbleness of a youngish man. I reckoned he was around medium height and build. In that dim light I had never even caught a glimpse of his features and, in retrospect, I hold a strong suspicion that the rascal had blackened his face. I thought of the chap who, in the face of our howling protests, had climbed the tree in broad daylight on May 10, when the osprey had just laid her first egg. He would have enjoyed the advantage of having climbed the tree before, yet that tree was probably among the easiest of stunted Scots pines in the Kingdom for anybody to climb. He would have known that the eggs would not hatch out until around the middle of June. He was also an egg-snatcher of the worst variety, as well as a man of courage. I reckoned the silhouette might have fitted him, but then it would have matched at least a million others, even if very, very few of them would have wished to lift a clutch of osprey eggs and fewer still would have known that a pair of these rare birds were nesting close by Loch Garten in that spring of 1958.

What had surprised most of us—myself in particular—was the time it had taken to reach the eyrie tree from the look-out. Reckoning it as about two hundred yards from the look-out to the eyrie tree and bearing in mind that we had missed intercepting the raider by certainly not more than fifty yards, if we could have had a hide mid-way between the look-out and the eyrie tree, the intruder would not have got away scot-free. Unfortunately it would have been impossible to reach such a hide without being seen by the incubating bird. The risk seemed too great at the time although, with the benefit of hindsight, I am sure that George will agree that it would have been a feasible proposition to man such a hide between last light and first light without disturbing the ospreys unduly. Even an unmanned hide, placed in such a position, might well have had deterrent value.

In hindsight, too, there is not much doubt that, long before the birds arrived, we should have sought permission to saw off all those lower boughs

A five-week-old osprey
(Bruce Coleman Limited)

of the eyrie tree. The tree might still have been climbable but it would have taken at least twice as long and the outcome might have been very different. It was all water under the bridge now but at least the bitter experience had taught us a few lessons.

We were still hopeful but disturbed by reports from one watcher after another that the dawn raid had clearly upset the ospreys. For weeks before the disturbance the sitting bird had been brooding steadily, usually only showing a handsome head above the rim. Now the bird seemed always to be alert and restless. Seeing was believing and, watching from the look-out on that afternoon what I saw did not please me at all. The dawn commotion had obviously upset both birds, but all that had happened twelve hours ago. Something was wrong and for the life of me I could not guess what.

That night I enjoyed a full night's sleep and forgot all about the birds. At breakfast next morning the marked change in their behaviour was the main topic of conversation. When I was on watch again in the afternoon George and Bert Axell came down to the look-out. We were greatly puzzled by the constant fidgeting of the incubating bird and, after a few minutes, George decided he could stand it no longer. Whilst I watched from the hide, he and Bert would nip out to the tree and take a look into the eyrie. A few nail-biting minutes ensued.

The osprey had left the nest almost as soon as they had emerged from the screen of trees and was flapping around, screaming peevishly. The next thing I saw was Bert Axell near the top of the tree. I held my breath. I saw him put a hand into the eyrie and extract something, after which he climbed down and was lost to sight. A minute or so afterwards I saw both emerge from the bushes and their woebegone faces showed that something was very wrong. It transpired that, looking into the nest with the benefit of full daylight, what Bert in the dim light of dawn had judged to be two osprey eggs were, in fact, two chicken eggs fairly skilfully daubed with brown shoe-polish to give them a rough resemblance to those of an osprey. At the foot of the eyrie tree they had found another smashed osprey egg containing a well-developed embryo. It was the end and we tasted in full measure the bitterness of utter defeat.

I had been on the go for the best part of forty-eight hours. I was now redundant and late that night I travelled south. The others remained and within a day or two they were watching the ospreys taking sticks to a pylon supporting high-tension cables about a mile from the old eyrie tree. This created no excitement because it was all part of the familiar pattern of behaviour when the ospreys' first nest had come to grief. Yet this time there was to be a difference. After they had taken only a few sticks to this pylon the birds suddenly switched their attentions to a tall Scots pine tree about four or five hundred yards to the east of Loch Garten and about a mile from the eyrie that had been raided. During the next six or seven days the birds built a substantial foundation to this new nest but it was now the middle of June, so nobody was surprised when they suddenly lost all interest in it and disappeared for the rest of the summer.

Throughout the previous weeks all our efforts had been concentrated on defending the eyrie from an attack. If we had failed it was not through want of trying and we only lost by the smallest of margins. At the time this did nothing to assuage the bitterness of defeat but, in retrospect, I derive quiet satisfaction from knowing that at the end of one of the worst night-vigils of my life I was not caught napping, that I saw, however vaguely in the dim light, that lowest bough waving violently and that I was sharp enough at once to realize that on that windless night this could only mean that some intruder was climbing the eyrie tree. None who were involved in the unsuccessful Operation Osprey, 1958, has any cause to feel ashamed.

CHAPTER TEN

Ospreys and Chickens

There were now two nests at Loch Garten: the big and quite ancient one that we had lately been watching and the embryo structure at the top of a tall Scots pine, a few hundred yards on the opposite side of the loch.

I could understand the reasons why George immediately began to make his plans around the eyrie which had already been used by the birds (not necessarily the same pair) more than once. In the first place we had never known the birds to show any interest in a 'frustration' eyrie in the following year. It is true that we only had two instances on which to make judgement—the 'frustration' eyrie beside the Sluggan Pass in 1955 and the other, in 1957, on the edge of Loch Morlich—but at the time it seemed a fair assumption that the ospreys would not choose the embryo eyrie to the east of Loch Garten in preference to the long-established one to the west.

One of the first things George did was to invoke a provision of the Protection of Birds Act 1954 which made it possible for either the Secretary of State or the Secretary of State for Scotland to declare an area as a bird reserve into which it would be an offence for all but authorized persons to enter. As all the land around Loch Garten was then owned by the Seafield Estates it was essential to get their agreement before approaching the Secretary of State. However, the Seafield Estates had already co-operated with genuine enthusiasm in our efforts and it was really no surprise when they willingly consented to the proposal.

Armed with this trump-card George Waterston was able to approach the powers-that-be in St Andrews House with confidence. Apart from the fact that George was a member of the Scottish Wild Birds Advisory Committee, there was never any reason to doubt that full co-operation would be forthcoming. The Order would be made long before the following spring, covering the area around the old eyrie on the marsh and extending eastward as far as the road that skirts the eastern fringe of the loch itself. Small notice-boards could then be put up at all the most likely points of entry, drawing the attention of the public to the fact that the area was a bird reserve and that any trespassers rendered themselves liable to prosecution. If this was unlikely to deter any determined egg-collector it would certainly strengthen the hands of the wardens and minimize casual intrusions.

I suppose it could have been argued that, in declaring this small area a bird reserve under the Act, some attention would be drawn to the site where the ospreys, we hoped, would be nesting but, following on the disastrous raid, the publicity in the press had been considerable, so that all those who were likely to harm the ospreys with malice aforethought were already 'in the know'.

All the lower boughs of the eyrie tree were carefully sawn off, flush with the trunk, early in the winter and the resulting scars treated to prevent the risk of rotting. The problem of covering the ground between the look-out and the eyrie tree reasonably quickly was more difficult. 1958 had not been a dry spring, yet it had not been a wet one, either, so that the marsh could have been much more waterlogged. George finally decided that the only answer lay in a good supply of wooden duck-boards and soon found a local carpenter who was prepared to produce several score of them before the end of the winter.

Any man of true mettle is not easily deterred from taking calculated risks. George had the difficult job of ensuring that, if the ospreys returned in 1959, the risks facing any would-be egg-thief had better be incalculable. His resolve strengthened by the testing fire of a bitter defeat and, no doubt, buoyed up by the knowledge that he was, by now, something of a seasoned campaigner in this osprey business, George set about his task in his usual thorough and methodical manner.

He began by ordering a fair quantity of barbed dannert wire, arranging for this to be delivered to the site. He mustered a bunch of volunteers and, over one week-end under his direction, the base of the eyrie tree was swathed in wire. The tall tree to the east of Loch Garten, in which the frustrated ospreys had built their embryo eyrie that was standing up well against the autumn and winter gales, also had the base of its trunk encoiled with what was left of the barbed-wire.

I was glad to discover that George was unhappy about the siting of our old Base Camp. I had always found it a depressing place, hemmed in by thick trees and damp to boot, although its handiness in relation to the look-out post was undeniable. However, George had been nosing around and discovered Inchdrein, a smallholding about half-a-mile due south of the look-out post where Miss Macdonald, a kind and warm-hearted woman, mothered a long series of incredibly lucky foster-children. This small croft, close by the lonely road that wound up over the Mains of Tulloch, was easily accessible by vehicle and yet was hidden away discretely enough for our purposes. Miss Macdonald had heard all about the ospreys and the disasters that had attended their efforts (and ours!) and was only too happy to allow us to site our new Base Camp adjacent to her house. Apart from the fact that, even on a cursory inspection in the depths of winter, this was a much more cheerful location than the old one, there were other advantages. There was plenty of water on tap for one thing and Miss Macdonald was on the telephone, for another.

George's next idea was to have some sort of communication between this new site for Base Camp and the man in the look-out. He must have been mindful of the fact that, had we had something of the kind the previous June, it would have been possible to alert those at Base Camp many minutes earlier than was the case, thus increasing the chances of catching any raider before he had made good his escape. George had friends everywhere and in this instance he had enlisted the aid of somebody in the army who had arranged a loan of some old but still serviceable field telephones and as much wire as was likely to be required. During the daytime, when only the watcher would be at the look-out post, it would be simple for him to ring for reinforcements, whilst the night-watchmen could raise a general alert at the twiddling of a handle. One man on a roster basis would doss down for the night in the caravan with the telephone beside him.

As the winter drew towards its end George had got most of his well-laid plans securely buttoned-up. The only real difficulty lay in the mustering of sufficient watchers to see the operation through to a successful conclusion. Operation Osprey 1959 differed from its predecessors in that George, quite rightly, did not propose to wait until the ospreys were obviously going to nest before launching the operation. Whilst it would not be necessary to introduce the onerous night-shifts until the laying of the first egg was imminent, the eyrie was to be watched throughout daylight as soon as the first bird returned to it. Judging by our previous experience that would be any time from the second week in April.

Whilst we could not afford to take on any 'old crocks', there was really no upper age limit for daytime watchers provided they were keen, physically fit and personally known to us. As it turned out we had a fairly easy task in recruiting enough to make it obvious that we were unlikely to run into serious difficulties on this score. This time we had to succeed after so many failures.

It was now that George Waterston had another of his brainwaves. We had always reckoned, during the hours of twilight and darkness at any rate, that a stint of three hours for a watcher working single-handed might fairly be reckoned a prudent limit of his endurance. However, we should now have two watchers on duty at night and, sharing the burden between them, the strain would really be more than halved. There was no reason why the change-over should not take place at the conclusion of four hours instead of the previous three. Thus the two watchers going on at ten o'clock in the evening would see it through till two in the morning, and their reliefs would carry on until six, a stint that would cover any thick mist which might persist for an hour or two after sunrise.

Osprey cock hovering over chick, Loch Garten eyrie, Speyside 1962
(Photograph by C. K. Mylne)

Nevertheless, we still found ourselves short of nocturnal manpower. It was a difficult decision to make because he had considerable responsibilities in his own area but George and I decided to get the late Eddie Balfour, then the RSPB's very able warden in the Orkneys, to join Operation Osprey 1959 for the first few weeks. Naturally enough, Eddie jumped at the offer like a hungry trout taking a mayfly and he proved to be a tower of strength in his quiet, self-effacing way. In the end, too, I once again approached Max Nicholson at the Nature Conservancy. With typical generosity and enthusiasm he assured me that he would help us out if it came to the pinch. So far as watchers were concerned, we were over the hump before the curtain went up.

In previous winters both George and I had fretted as to whether or not the ospreys would return in the following spring. I daresay that we occasionally had our qualms on this score but, in that long, well-planned lead-up to Operation Osprey, 1959, I cannot recollect that we ever voiced them. Before the end of March George had everything planned to the last detail. The vanguard of the brigade of watchers already had their marching orders. Material for the new and bigger look-out, telephones and drums of cable, tents, beds, pots and pans and all the other necessary supplies were already in store at Inchdrein. In spite of the dismal record, it seemed outrageous to harbour any doubts as to whether or not the birds would play ball yet, after all this detailed and meticulous planning involving the expenditure of much time and energy, we must have known that if they failed to do so then we had set up one of the biggest anti-climaxes in the long history of bird protection.

As soon as April came George was up at Inchdrein with one or two volunteers, in order to have everything in readiness before the birds arrived. There was much to be done, not least the laying of the telephone wire between the caravan at the new Base Camp at Inchdrein and the look-out. In places the insulated wiring had to be run high up between trees on either side of any used track or lane; it was the kind of job, especially in bitterly cold, windy weather, which nobody would like to do twice. However, George eventually telephoned from Inchdrein to inform me that the stage was well and truly set and that the opera could begin just as soon as the two principal performers arrived.

We had not long to wait. George rang me on April 18 to tell me that one osprey, almost certainly the cock bird, had arrived at Loch Garten that day. This bird had apparently shown some interest in the 'frustration' eyrie of the previous summer but there were no grounds for worry on this score. Once the female joined the cock the birds would surely revert to the long-established site.

A few days later I got a nice admixture of good and bad news. The female had joined the male on April 22 and the pair were actively building up the remains of the frustration eyrie, ignoring all the advantages of the adjacent bird reserve, newly declared for their especial benefit.

All preparations had been made and laid for the proper reception and protection of the old eyrie. The new and enlarged look-out was already in position. It was more than a cut above its predecessors. It was, in fact, a sectional hut of considerable size. Although not all that easy to handle, the hut had been made in sections that could be bolted together with reasonable ease. A long chain of heavy, wooden duck-boards stretched across the boggy marsh from the look-out to this eyrie tree. The field telephones had been laid and tested. The task of shifting them to accommodate the demands of Operation Osprey if the birds insisted on using this new site were formidable indeed.

There was time enough yet for the birds to change their minds. There was still the last week of April in hand and, the previous year, the female had not laid her first egg until May 10. George rightly decided to 'play it cool', even if he had never before watched a pair of ospreys determinedly building up an embryo eyrie in the month of April. If the ospreys were really going to use this new site it might prove fatal to disturb them unduly whilst they were engaged in feverishly adding huge sticks and bits of moss and heather to the growing structure. At least this hiatus gave George ample opportunity to consider the possibilities of the developing situation and the problems it would pose if the birds were to be adequately protected at this new location. How George must have blessed his own foresight in having swathed the base of this new eyrie tree with many coils of barbed dannert wire. And, apart from this protective wire, this new tree was not only twice the height of the old one but also much more difficult to climb.

This new eyrie was situated several hundred yards to the east-nor'-east of the road where it skirts the edge of Loch Garten. It was virtually invisible from the highway itself, certainly to the extent that it was never likely to be noticed by any passer-by, but it could be surveyed, together with the surrounding marsh in which the tree stood on a broad patch of higher and drier ground, from a clearing in a piece of thick forestry on a steeply rising hill about a mile to the south. There was an old peat road, gated and padlocked, leading up from the public road beside the loch. This roughish track was reasonably firm and wound its way very conveniently towards the new eyrie tree, at first through a cover of trees, followed by an open stretch through heather and other ground scrub, after which it dipped slightly into more trees that screened it from the eyrie, petering out, together with the tree-cover, about two hundred yards short of the eyrie tree itself. This peat road was not difficult to negotiate with the Dormobile or a land-rover but if an osprey were on the eyrie the bird would be able to see the vehicle during a part of its journey, as well as hearing it—the noise being emphasized by the constant gear-changing that would be necessary. On foot it would be possible to reach the fringe of the trees nearest the eyrie tree without being either seen or heard by a bird on the nest.

George certainly had problems and these were accentuated by the unexpected speed with which the ospreys got on with the job of completing their new home. At the end of three or four days the eyrie had developed into a substantial structure of dead sticks and the male bird was bringing in great talons-full of moss and bits of heather and presenting them to the female who was already busy lining the nest. There was no longer any reason to doubt that the female would lay her eggs in this new eyrie; furthermore, it seemed probable that she was going to lay her first egg considerably earlier than she had done in 1958. We could not, of course, be sure that this pair were the same. Some of us had watched the 1958 pair at close range over long periods but the fact that they looked familiar and that their general behaviour was similar in many respects is no proof of identity. On the other hand the reappearance of the cock in the area at least suggests that he was the old bird, especially as he settled in on the 'frustration' eyrie without hesitation. And the speed with which the female, on joining him, had got down to the business of building up the remains of this embryo nest inclines one to the belief that she, too, had been here before.

Almost everything that had been done to protect the old eyrie tree now had to be undone. It was as laborious and time-consuming to pick up over a hundred heavy duck-boards as it had been to lay them down in the first place, but now they had to be loaded into a vehicle, transported over two miles and then unloaded behind the last screen of trees near the new eyrie, ready to be laid down again, a few at a time, either when both ospreys were temporarily absent or in the late evening twilight when the eyrie tree was untenanted. It was simple enough to gather up about half-a-mile of telephone line, but the relaying between Inchdrein and the new site was quite another matter. The distance involved was almost three times as great, so a lot more wire had to be obtained in a hurry. So far as possible the new line was laid along the most direct route between Inchdrein and the eyrie but some diversions were essential, as when it was necessary to carry it under the public road by the loch by making use of a culvert. The successful laying of this cable occupied several persons for the better part of three long days. The dismantling of the sectional wooden hut and its reassembly at the new site was relatively easy. The transporting of the large sections between one site and the other, involving the borrowing of a trailer, was much more difficult and, on some of the rougher sections of the route, decidedly hazardous.

I went up to Speyside for a few days at the end of April and was both impressed and agreeably surprised to find the preparations had been more or less completed, in spite of the sudden change in the plans due to the waywardness of the ospreys. I must mention a person who contributed greatly to Operation Osprey, 1959. I had fairly recently recruited Frank Hamilton on to the staff of the RSPB. He was then a young man and just about as enthusiastic and hard-working as they come. Frank is one of the most cheerful characters I have ever met; he was the sort of irrepressible chap who could even laugh at his own weariness—a morale-booster if ever there was one, ever willing to shoulder more than his fair share of the work. When George Waterston retired as Director of the RSPB in Scotland, it was Frank Hamilton who succeeded him.

My arrival at the end of April coincided with the start of the round-the-clock watches. I had the good luck to be on duty with Eddie Balfour, whom I knew very well, when the female osprey roosted on the eyrie for the first time on the night of April 29–30 and the cock slept on a dead tree nearby. It was wonderful to see these truly magnificent birds in action once again. The new hide was both roomy and storm-proof. Wooden slats could be lowered inwards to give perfect views of the eyrie and its immediate surroundings. One could sit on a firm cross-bench with one's companion and there was a bar so placed that elbows could be rested on it whilst using binoculars. There was an oil-stove which warmed this look-out hut on any cold, frosty night and on which one could also boil a kettle, albeit rather slowly, to make warming draughts of tea or coffee. By comparison with the previous year, anyway, it was luxury.

Eddie and I took stints of about half-an-hour each. Being the end of April, it was dark by ten o'clock but the thought of all that barbed dannert wire coiled round the base of the tree certainly added to our confidence. The worst period for watching on dark nights would be before midnight. This new eyrie tree was situated to the north-east of the look-out, so that the first glint of dawn would throw it into strong silhouette, clearly an advantage in countering any raid at first light.

Towards midnight, when it was quite dark, Eddie and I suddenly had our confidence badly shattered. A light shone away beyond the eyrie and then was turned off. Somebody was out on the marsh, using a strong torch. We strained our eyes but could see nothing in the inky blackness. We could not hear anything either but we did not think that the osprey had left the eyrie. Perhaps the intruder was too far off to disturb her. Then the torchlight was visible again, winking on and off once or twice. We were just thinking of ringing Inchdrein on the field telephone and sounding the alarm when, thank goodness, the penny dropped. I realized that the lights were caused by a car threading its way along a road several miles away, appearing only intermittently because of the many big stands of trees. At least we were able to warn subsequent watchers not to panic unduly!

It was with a heavy heart that I went south by train on the following evening. After the failure of the previous year I would have wished to have played a full part in the present operation but George had plenty of stalwart watchers and I had no possible excuse to desert my desk. I had, however, arranged to take a fortnight's leave early in June and hoped to be in on the show round about the time when, if all went well, the eggs could be expected to hatch. The fact that the female had sat on the eyrie on that long night of April 29–30 might have suggested that she had already laid her first egg even though she had only been present for seven days. However, I heard later that she had not been on the nest the following night, although she was never absent at night after that. It would seem almost certain, therefore, that she laid her first egg on May 1.

All the news that reached me in London was good. When, at the end of the third week in May, I heard that all was still progressing well, I began to count the days with growing impatience. Reckoning that the incubation period, as stated in *The Handbook of British Birds*, lasted for 35 days and assuming that incubation started immediately after the female had laid her first egg on May 1, the first chick might be expected to hatch on June 4. About noon on that day Peter Allpress, David Harrison, my wife and I set off from London with the prospect of watching the ospreys for a fortnight at what must surely be one of the most exciting and interesting periods of their breeding cycle. All three of us men were going to undertake our share of the watches whilst Caroline was coming along to cook for the mob. She was a great asset because she happens to be a very good cook. The weather was warm and uncommonly dry. After an overnight stop in Penrith, we were away early the next morning, lunched in Stirling and then travelled on to Kingussie, where I had arranged to meet George at 'The Star' at six o'clock so that we could all enjoy a dinner together before covering the last few miles to Loch Garten. I quote the following long passage from what I wrote in a book, *The Return of the Osprey*:

The new and improved hide from which we kept watch
(Photograph by C. K. Mylne)

'When we arrived in Kingussie about six o'clock I found a note from George. He could not get over to dine with us because they were having a bit of a celebration at Base Camp. The chicks had already hatched. Never was there quite such a mixture of splendid and disappointing news. However, we duly drank a toast to the health of the young ospreys, though I have the deepest suspicions that they were still in their shells at the time.

'When we got to Base Camp it was difficult to get any sense out of anybody. Apart from the two unfortunates on watch, the caravan was crowded. In a good imitation of a sort of caravan Babel, we were told that if we would shut up we should hear a recording of the osprey chick which had hatched within the past twenty-four hours. Bob Wade, from the B.B.C., had obtained this perhaps unique record. The recording gear was set up, one window of the caravan being broken in the process. We were told to listen for a grunting sound. We duly heard it, loud and distinct. It seemed an odd sound for a newly-hatched bird to make, but as we had never heard young osprey chicks in voice, who were we, newcomers, to cast doubts on its authenticity? There was unanimous agreement amongst all the old and experienced hands that at least one osprey chick was safely out of its shell. We drank more toasts to its everlasting happiness and wandered off to our various tents to make up our beds and settle down for the night.

'The events of the next few days puzzled many of us. A parabolic reflector had been located at the foot of the eyrie tree and was connected to earphones in the look-out hide. One object of this was to enable the watchers on duty on dark or misty nights to detect any strange sounds near the eyrie tree. The microphone was extremely sensitive. When the hen bird shuffled about in the nest some forty feet above it the noise made was quite terrific. Any person moving in the heather near the foot of the tree sounded like an elephant however cautiously they might try to move. Peter Allpress and I took the watch on the morning of Saturday, 6th June. The hen seemed rather restless, though she brooded throughout most of our four-hour watch. Once she seemed to peck for a long time in the bottom of the nest, as if she might be eating fragments of eggshell. On another occasion she flew off to get a stick which she brought back to the eyrie and as she landed I thought for a moment that I saw the head of a tiny chick. This was wishful thinking, for one has not the remotest hope of seeing a newly-hatched chick from an angle well below the rim of the nest and I am glad, on looking up the log-book, to see that I wrote: "I suppose it *must* have been a bit of moss or something blowing up in the wind. But it did look like crown of small chick."

'Late that afternoon, and over thirty hours after the first chick was believed to have hatched out, the cock flew in with a fish, gave it to the hen on the eyrie and she flew off to eat it on a nearby tree, the male standing guard on the nest. This was the pattern of behaviour which had persisted throughout the whole period of incubation. There was no question of the hen giving any food to a chick on that day.

'The behaviour the next day, Sunday, 7th June, was exactly the same. When the cock came in with a fish the hen took it away to feed on it. No food was passed to any young chick. It is well known that often birds of prey do not feed their chicks for some time after the hatch has taken place, but some of us found it more and more difficult to believe that a chick which hatched on Friday morning had still not apparently been given a morsel by the Sunday evening, although plenty of food was available. I was on watch the following night and several times after sunrise I recorded hearing very thin piping "cheeps" over the microphone. I was uncertain as to whether these came from a chick in the nest, but on balance I rather think they did. All that day, however, the other observers reported no signs of any food being passed to a chick, no definite change in the normal pattern of behaviour and no calls heard which could reasonably be attributed to a chick.

'I found the situation so intriguing that I decided to go on watch again that night. Peter Allpress and Humphrey ap-Evans, the falconer, were my good companions. About 1.30 on the morning of Tuesday, 9th June, we recorded curious crunching noises over the earphones, coupled with repeated thin peeps. The piping sounds were indeed so thin that ap-Evans could not hear them. By five o'clock the piping sounds were clearer. Peter and I were confident now that they came from an osprey chick and we were relieved when, at last, ap-Evans admitted to hearing them too. At about this time the cock came in with a fish, but for the first time the hen failed to take the fish from him, remaining on the eyrie, the cock eventually flying off with the fish to a nearby tree. But then the cock returned with the partly-eaten fish and this time the hen took it and flew off with it, leaving the cock to brood for nearly an hour. We finished our watch at nine o'clock, having heard the thin piping sounds again and again, but we never saw any food passed to a chick. If in fact it had only been emerging from the shell during the past twenty-four hours this was perhaps not unreasonable. Peter and I found it impossible to believe that a chick which hatched early on a Friday was still alive but unfed four days later. We still hold that view.

'Later that day others watched the hen behaving on several occasions as if she were feeding a chick. Now, too, the whole pattern of the behaviour of the pair underwent a significant change. When the cock came in with a fish she no longer took it from him and flew off, leaving him to brood. She remained with the fish, feeding herself on the eyrie and passing small morsels to the young. The cock might remain beside her for a few minutes, then usually flew off to a nearby perch until she had finished eating and settled to brood again. He then usually flew up to the nest, seized the remains of the fish and took them with him back to his perch to feed himself.

'The actual date of the hatch must, perhaps, remain a matter of opinion and opinions are sharply divided between 4th–5th June and 8th–9th June. If it was not a young osprey chick, what was the curious noise which Bob Wade had so faithfully recorded? On the other hand, is it reasonable to suppose that the chick waited over four days before receiving any food? And there is one final point which is relevant. If the first chick hatched on 4th or 5th June then the incubation period was noticeably shorter in 1959 than in either 1960 or 1961. Relevant but, alas! not conclusive. The debate can go on until kingdom come. Knowing the protagonists I fancy that, off and on, it probably will.'

I can only add that I still hold firmly to my belief that not one of the eggs had hatched on June 5, 1959. I think that it was likely that the first chick was pecking its way out of a chipped egg on the Sunday, June 7, and that at least one chick was clear of its shell on the night of June 8–9. Steady incubation may well not have begun until the female settled down on the nest at twilight on May 1, so that May 2 might reasonably be adjudged the first day of incubation. If the hatch began on June 7 or 8, the incubation period lasted 37 or 38 days, which is what one might have expected.

Now that there were chicks in the nest the male dropped his selfish habit of feeding himself first, bringing the fish straight up to the eyrie, presenting it to the hen and then retiring to one of his several perches on the marsh. One could watch the female carefully stripping off bits of flesh from the fish and feeding the chicks; not until the growing appetites of the young were satisfied did she start feeding herself.

Later in the summer, when the appetites of the young ospreys increased with their size, the male might bring in as many as five or six fish in a single day but even in mid-June he would produce two or three, going off hunting again before midday and coming back with his prey about one or two o'clock, after which he took a longish siesta before departing again early in the evening. Sometimes he returned with his last fish of the day as late as nine or ten o'clock. Unlike the incubation period, once the ospreys had young in the nest the duller moments seldom lasted for long and one was always on the alert in order not to miss whatever might happen next.

Occasionally, if the cock had been absent for a considerable time, the brooding female would start crying rather peevishly. More often than not I reckoned that this effort was largely wasted because the cock must have been far beyond earshot. However, quite often when the hen called in this way the cock would appear within a very few minutes, carrying a fish in his talons. Perhaps the female, with the advantage of her high and wide viewpoint, had spotted her mate long before he entered our more limited visual range.

Quiet moments were sometimes interrupted by the appearance of a crow or a buzzard. If the male osprey were present he would be on to a crow at once, soon seeing the marauder off the premises. Buzzards could create uproar. Both ospreys would often go into attack and the intruders, hardly renowned for their courage, would beat a hasty retreat. I am sorry that I missed one or two spectacular dog-fights between the ospreys and the odd golden eagle that wandered into their territory. For all their size and majesty, golden eagles have always struck me, if I may be excused the anthropomorphism, of being rather

Silhouetted against the fading light, an osprey brings in the last fish of the day (Photograph by Tom Weir)

cowardly at heart and certainly they were no match for the swashbuckling ospreys. As birds of prey, ospreys are not particularly aggressive but if any other bird is spoiling for a fight they are welcome!

I shall always remember those halcyon June days of 1959 when one could still watch the ospreys and their family in privacy and yet enjoy the company of good friends and colleagues and have a lot of quiet fun. Before our first week was over we reckoned that there were two chicks in the eyrie. Then followed two or three days when we suspected that there might be a third young bird but could not be sure. Anyone who has ever tried to count tiny beaks appearing and disappearing at feeding time above the rim of an osprey eyrie 200 yards away will be able to appreciate our difficulties. However, by the middle of June there was no doubt about it! The ospreys had hatched out three lusty young and our cup of happiness was brimful.

In operations of this kind it is never safe to presume upon ultimate success. With a rather heavy heart I left the area with my party on June 20, which was a Saturday, warm and brilliantly sunny. We all dined together in Stirling, where my wife and I said goodbye to Peter Allpress and David Harrison, who were travelling on to Edinburgh where Peter had a business engagement on the Monday, whilst we had booked sleepers on the night train to Euston. We were in London quite early on the Sunday morning, took a taxi to Waterloo, reaching our home in Hampshire about midday.

At one o'clock I switched on the radio to listen to the news and was horrified to hear that a big forest fire was raging in the neighbourhood of Nethybridge, not much more than a mile from the eyrie. It was a hot enough day anyway, but these tidings raised my temperature still higher. I am bound to admit that the information that the fire, fanned by a fair breeze, might threaten some of the homes in Nethybridge seemed to me, at that particular moment, largely irrelevant. I pictured in my mind's eye thick palls of smoke pouring over the marsh, blotting out the view of the eyrie, suffocating the chicks and causing the old birds to desert. There was a lot of heather and scrub on that marsh and it was tinder-dry. If this had caught fire, what hope was there of saving the eyrie tree? For all I knew to the contrary, it might already be in flames. In all our long efforts to safeguard the ospreys we had been dogged by a fair amount of bad luck. Was this to be the final straw? I quote what I wrote in *The Return of the Osprey*, when this near-disastrous happening was rather fresher in my mind than it is now:

> 'A south-easterly wind fanned the flames and blew the fire across the narrow barrier of a road running from Tulloch to Nethybridge. It transpired that the watchers on duty had seen the dense columns of smoke earlier and telephoned back to Base Camp. Every man except those on watch had turned out in the grilling heat to fight the fire. Frank Hamilton, who was one of the watchers at the time, tells the story in a very laconic way. "We fought the fire like blazes to try to prevent its getting nearer to the ospreys. The wind was south-east, which made our task more difficult. Luckily the wind shifted when we were just about whacked. Everything was O.K. then, the fire driving on in almost the opposite direction to the osprey nest, straight towards Nethybridge village."'

My impression was that Frank, at the time, was as little worried about the fate of Nethybridge as I had myself been when I first heard the bad news on the wireless, although I am glad to be able to report that no harm came either to the lives or the buildings of the inhabitants of that small but delightful place.

Within a day or two I had yet another shock, even if it was of a very different nature. I was working at my desk in the offices of the RSPB in London when

George came through on the telephone from Inchdrein. He proceeded to explain to me, at some length, one of the most scatterbrained notions that I had ever heard. George began by pointing out that one way and another, including the publicity given to the whole affair by the news about the forest fire, a great many people would probably come to Loch Garten to try to see the ospreys. I reckoned that might be so, but we had plenty of watchers to police the site and nobody could drive up to it because we had a padlock on that five-barred gate. George explained that he had no intention of allowing anybody to drive up in a vehicle to the look-out. He had no intention of permitting any members of the public to go into the look-out at all. His plan was to erect a screen to the rear of the look-out, well-hidden by small trees yet affording a clear view of the eyrie itself and invite members of the public to walk up the peat road from the loch, take a peep at the birds through a special pair of high-powered binoculars and invite them to give a small donation to the funds. It was sheer lunacy. I supposed it was the hot weather that had driven poor George off his nut!

George reasoned that it was far better to have a hundred or more folk properly organized, walking to and from the public hide by a well-trodden path over which the ospreys had become accustomed to a lot of movement, including the odd car, than for one or two people to come wandering on to the marsh from the side opposite the look-out, disturbing both birds and watchers alike. Reluctantly I conceded that he had a point, yet I was still dubious. Once we publicized the site of the eyrie in the press and elsewhere there could be no going back. The cat would be well and truly out of the bag. It would be far better, I suggested, if we kept quiet for the rest of the summer, dealt with any curious trespassers to the best of our ability and gave ourselves time to consider what we might do the next season in this matter of public access.

George was not to be fobbed off. He considered the risks negligible and reckoned that any publicity for the ospreys was bound to be good for their future success. He wanted to go ahead with the idea right away. However, he had rung me up because he wanted to get my agreement. If I did not agree with the new plan he was not prepared to go ahead with it and that would be that—but he hastened to add that, in his considered opinion, we should have missed a great opportunity to promote the protection of rare birds. As he was dead keen to go ahead, what he really meant was that, if I vetoed his plans, it was I who would have missed the opportunity. George was a canny lad and no mistake.

Whilst I am not especially eager, by nature, to make decisions on the spur of the moment unless it is necessary, I am even more strongly opposed to procrastination. It was clear that George was not asking for my advice in this particular matter. He knew exactly what he wished to do and he believed it was right. Because I was the boss of the outfit he was paying me the courtesy of obtaining my consent—or otherwise. I had known George for many years. It was through my recommendation, after all, that he had been made Scottish Representative of the RSPB in the first place. Either full or part-time, he had now been working for the Society for six years. I reckoned that if he did not know what he was doing then, logically, I did not know what I was doing, either. I told him to go ahead with his wildcat scheme—and the best of Scottish luck to him. I replaced the telephone and sat back to draw breath, wondering if I, too, had taken leave of my senses. The public were to be invited to come to Loch Garten to take a look at the rarest breeding birds in Britain as if the whole thing were just a bloody peep-show . . .

George got cracking without delay. Within a few days it was announced in the press and over the radio that the public could see the ospreys between ten o'clock in the morning and seven o'clock in the evening. George arranged that, during these hours, one watcher would be on duty in the look-out and another would be engaged on marshalling the visitors at the public look-out and explaining what was happening, as well as shaking a collecting-box under their noses before they finally wandered back down the peat road. George's decision to show the ospreys to the general public was undoubtedly right, yet I'll bet my bottom dollar that he never dreamt that no less than 14,000 of them would take advantage of this offer during the next seven weeks—an average of 300 visitors per day. And I had thought of it as a scatterbrained notion: Oh! well, don't they say that genius is akin to madness?

A few weeks after this new and highly successful scheme had been put into operation I travelled up to Speyside to see how it was working. It was, in fact, working very well yet I should be dishonest if I did not confess that I disliked what I saw. On fine week-ends, between the early morning and early evening, as many as a thousand people would troop up the peat road in bunches of twos and threes or more and await their turn by the caravan to take a look at the ospreys through the high-powered glasses. Some of the visitors had never used binoculars before and had to be guided through the simple drill whilst others waited with varying degrees of impatience to get their peep. The ospreys were completely accustomed to seeing movements on the short, exposed stretch of the peat road. Apart from this, the many visitors were out of their sight and the birds were not in any way disturbed. All the time visitors were present there was a low murmur of conversation. It was a relief, so far as I was concerned, when the gate by the road was closed and padlocked in the evening and one could once more have the ospreys to oneself and watch them in the proper peace and quiet of their lovely surroundings. One could do the same thing early in the mornings, before the first car pulled up in the park by the loch and disgorged the vanguard of a long series of sightseers. The glorious pioneer days were over, so far as the ospreys were concerned, and I felt rather sorry yet I was left in no doubt whatsoever that, in the interests of bird-protection in general and of the ospreys in particular, George Waterston had done the right thing in opening up the site to the general public once the really hazardous period was over for the season and there were healthy chicks in the eyrie.

The 'peep-show' in full swing
(Photograph by C. K. Mylne)

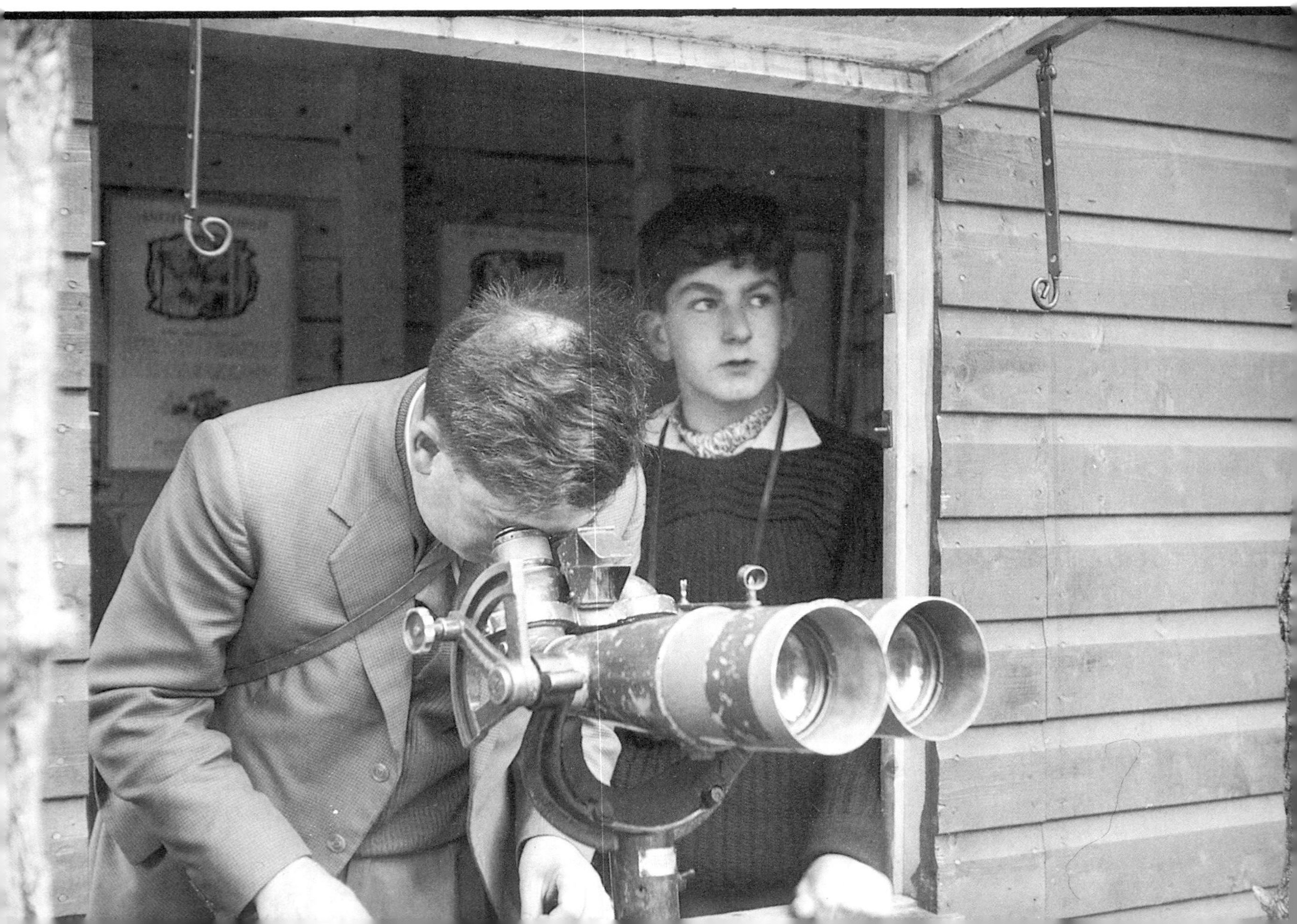

CHAPTER ELEVEN

Harvest of the Years

There were good grounds for rejoicing at the end of that summer of 1959, when the pair of ospreys and their three young went south to their winter quarters. It was not until the young birds finally left the eyrie in August that George Waterston and all those who had assisted in the effort could let out a long sigh of relief and really 'count their chickens'. And that long-awaited triumph happened just over four years after the discovery of the frustration eyrie in the Sluggan Pass had set us all on fire. This potty little Sluggan nest was, after all, the first evidence we had that a pair of ospreys were present in Speyside. The few of us who were 'in the know' felt certain, at that time, that ospreys would soon be re-established in the Highlands. If optimism is necessary to stoke the fire of enthusiasm, it is fairly obvious, in retrospect, that we were too optimistic by half.

In that first long winter of waiting, the disclosure that a pair of ospreys had successfully reared young in 1954 fuelled our hopes. The three summers of frustration that followed served not only to cut us all down to size but taught us the nature of the problem and provided the experience, however hard, that led to ultimate triumph.

After the successful nesting in 1954, there is no reason to doubt that a pair were present in 1955 and laid eggs. Once we appreciated the significance of a frustration-eyrie like that one in the Sluggan, this much was plain. Judging by the date when the birds were first discovered playing about in the Sluggan, the ospreys had lost their eggs, although the cause of this disaster remains unknown. In 1956 they had again attempted to nest, but in 1957 it seems at least probable that only one bird was present. In 1958, when we had watched the old eyrie at Loch Garten round-the-clock, we were very close to our goal. If we had only had more experience of ospreys we might well have succeeded. This does not detract from the daring and courage displayed by the unknown person who raided the eyrie at first light. Yet there were certainly no victors in that nightmare: the raider failed; we failed and the ospreys failed, too. The handful of us who were deeply involved in this osprey business were all comparatively young men at that time and four years of failure seemed like an eternity. If the successful breeding of the ospreys in 1959, when all three young birds were launched into their futures, engendered a mood of euphoria which was scarcely justified by this one great event, our mood of renewed optimism was understandable enough. As things turned out, it was justified.

Good fun though they were, the years of inadequacy and improvisation were over. The Royal Society for the Protection of Birds had more than doubled its support, so that more money was at long last available to finance vital projects, of which Operation Osprey was certainly one. The plans George laid during the winter of 1959–60 were concentrated on the Loch Garten site. Local accommodation had been obtained for the watchers and relays of volunteers were engaged to cook for them. There would be enough watchers to ensure that their periods of duty would not be too prolonged and there would be 'rest-days' for them when they could get much-needed exercise exploring the forests or hills, enjoying a bit of bird-watching free from constant anxiety. By the use of electronic and other devices, it was also made much more difficult for any would-be raider to attempt to scale the eyrie-tree without alerting the sentries long before he could reach the nest, let alone escape with his booty.

In 1960 the male arrived back at the eyrie on April 8, the female joining him ten days later. If there was no certainty that they were the same pair as in the previous year, there was strong circumstantial evidence that they were because their behaviour seemed so similar, the male again making use of his old roosting-perches and so on. Perhaps it did not matter overmuch. What was important was that they reared two young and were seen by over 20,000 members of the public, compared with 14,000 in the previous summer. The ospreys were 'on the map', attracting tourists to an area much in need of them, so that, by local standards, conservation had become big business. Public opinion was very much on the side of the ospreys and public opinion, whether we like to admit it or not, is always much more effective than the law.

The Loch Garten eyrie has been used by the ospreys in every subsequent summer, mostly successfully. In the winter of 1960–1 some person, or persons unknown, took the trouble to saw a considerable way through the trunk of the eyrie-tree, not far above ground-level. By any standards, this was a malicious act, the only possible motive being to weaken the tree so that it might fall in a heavy gale. Winter or not, George never visited Speyside without visiting the eyrie, with all the possibilities it then held for the successful re-establishment of the ospreys in the Scottish Highlands. He soon discovered what had occurred and took steps to strengthen the trunk of the Scots pine with metal struts. It is still standing today and by 1978 the number of visitors had grown to around three-quarters of a million.

In 1963 the Loch Garten eyrie was blown out of the tree in a gale, whilst in 1971 the nest was robbed. In most summers, however, the birds using this eyrie have bred successfully so that after twenty years of use, almost forty young ospreys have been reared at this site. In 1963 a pair of ospreys were nesting at another site, so that at long last the tide appeared to have turned. Four years later, in 1967, three pairs were breeding. By 1969 this figure had grown to four and at least twenty-three young ospreys had been reared to the free-flying stage during the previous ten years.

We have travelled a long way from the pioneer days of the late 1950s. In 1976, by which time at least 142 ospreys had been reared in Scotland since the birds had staged their post-war come-back, the RSPB stated at the end of one of their handouts to visitors to the Loch Garten eyrie that 'the outlook for these superb fish-eating birds is bright'. I believe that is a fair assessment of the future prospects and it is one which must give a lot of satisfaction to all those who laboured so hard and unselfishly during the four frustrating summers following the successful breeding of ospreys in 1954—efforts that culminated in triumph in 1959. Those were rough-and-ready, makeshift days, when manpower was usually at a premium, so that the going was often hard and there were times when even the fittest of men had to be called on to exceed what I think might fairly be regarded as the prudent limits of human endurance.

It is sad to recall that many of those early pioneers—my old friend J. K. Stanford is but one example—are no longer with us. Yet if they laid the foundations of a most successful enterprise, all that has been achieved would have been impossible but for the dedicated enthusiasm of those who followed them. If all who had given their services could be mentioned in this book it would fill many pages. If one salutes them, one and all, it is possible to mention only a few. Apart from those already referred to, there was Wing-Commander Dick Fursman, who, after the successful nesting in 1959, was willingly pressed into very active service by George. For several years Dick assumed the considerable responsibility of O.C., Speyside Osprey Troops, and we could not have found a better man for this job. Another acquisition in those comparatively early years of the campaign was Roy Dennis, yet another tireless, selfless character who came to the RSPB from the Fair Isle Bird Observatory and who is now the Society's Highland Officer. Douglas Weir has been another tower of strength over a long period. Under the supervision of Roy, Douglas and Harvey Burton—both of whom are able to climb trees like monkeys—have helped in the ringing of many young ospreys. The results of this work is invaluable and, as it continues over the years it will shed more and more light on the fortune of our Scottish ospreys during the long period when they leave their breeding-grounds and we can do little or nothing, directly, to safeguard them. At least 15 young Scottish ospreys have been recovered abroad. These have been dead birds and, alas! there is not much room to doubt that most had been deliberately destroyed. It must also be borne in mind that when a ringed bird is deliberately killed, perhaps more especially in the case of birds of prey, only an unknown percentage are likely to be returned through the official channels.

More ringing of young osprey chicks—coupled, one must add, with more destruction, mostly illegal, of the birds bearing the rings—will almost certainly provide much valuable information about our Highland ospreys in future years. In the meanwhile the results already to hand are extremely interesting and surely give us at least some indication of the general area in which many of our Scottish ospreys spend the winter. I am indebted to Robert Spencer and Robert Hudson of the British Trust of Ornithology for supplying the ensuing information. Within the British Isles twelve ospreys have been recovered—all having been ringed in Sweden—over the years from 1942–1978. Outside the British Isles the following ringed Scottish birds have been found: one bird in both 1967 and 1968 in Spain; in 1971 one in Portugal and two in Mauritania; in 1973 one in Senegal; in 1974 one in Portugal, Gambia and Norway; in 1976 another in Spain; in 1977 no birds were recovered abroad. George Waterston brought to my notice the extraordinary case of a Scottish chick ringed in 1976, recovered at sea on a fishing boat on April 25, 1978, west of Latrabjarg, N.W. Iceland (where the species has never been known to breed), and taken to Reykjavik and released on April 30. It was found dead on May 22, 1978, at Stora Burfell, N.W. Iceland.

All those of us who, at some time or another, have been deeply involved in Operation Osprey are only too well aware of the great part played by George

An RSPB warden holding a chick after having carefully ringed it
(Photograph by C. K. Mylne)

Waterston. It was not simply a matter of his organizational ability nor the disposition of his limited troops in the early years of the campaign; it was his dogged courage and determination, his congenital inability to accept defeat when all seemed lost, that inspired so many of us to fight against the odds.

This book should have been written by George. It would have been, too, had he not been stricken down by ill health, to survive which he has had to call on his own indomitable fighting qualities and the selfless love and devotion of his wife Irene. I was only asked to write this book as a substitute. I must accept the responsibility for any shortcomings in this story of our Scottish ospreys. That drawback apart, I shall rest happy if it both entertains and informs readers about one of the greatest achievements in bird-conservation and, at the same time, shows what a great debt we all owe to George himself.

In the ultimate analysis, however, we must not forget the Royal Society for the Protection of Birds. This great Society can now boast well over a quarter-of-a-million members, yet only 25 years ago, when Operation Osprey first began, its supporters were numbered in four figures! The RSPB maintains many important bird reserves. Not long after the ospreys had established themselves at Loch Garten, the RSPB purchased 1517 acres of land surrounding Mallachie and Garten, thus not only safeguarding the future of the nesting ospreys, but permanently establishing an important bird reserve for many species, including the crested tit. For the wardening and maintenance of existing reserves and for the establishment of new ones the Society both needs and deserves the support of all those who can afford a comparatively modest annual subscription. I daresay that many readers of this book will have joined the Society long ago but it may persuade others to join by writing to the Director of the RSPB at The Lodge, Sandy, Bedfordshire, for particulars.

I close this account with a year-by-year table showing how the ospreys have increased and flourished since those first post-war Speyside birds led us such a merry dance. It is a record which is, in itself, a tribute to the RSPB, as well as affording much encouragement for all who hope that one of our finest birds of prey will continue to flourish in Britain as the years roll on.

Ospreys in Scotland since 1954

(Reproduced by courtesy of the RSPB)

Year	*Pairs Breeding*	*Successful*	*Failed*	*Total Young Reared*	*(Loch Garten)*
1954	1	1	0	2	—
1955	1	0	1	0	—
1956	1	0	1	0	—
1957	0	0	0	0	—
1958	1	0	1	0	—
1959	1	1	0	3	3
1960	1	1	0	2	2
1961	1	1	0	3	3
1962	1	1	0	1	1
1963	2	0	2	0	0
1964	2	1	1	3	3
1965	2	1	1	1	1
1966	2	0	2	0	0
1967	3	2	1	5	3
1968	3	2	1	5	2
1969	4	3	1	6	2
1970	6	3	3	8	3
1971	7	5	2	11	0
1972	12	6	6	14	2
1973	13	10	3	21	2
1974	14	10	4	21	3
1975	9	7	2	16	0
1976	14	10	4	20	2
1977	*c.* 15	6	*c.* 9	12	2
1978	22	11	11	*c.* 20	3

Select Bibliography

BAXTER, E. V. and RINTOUL, L. J. (1953), *The Birds of Scotland*

BENT, A. C. (1937), *Life Histories of North American Birds of Prey*

BROWN, L. (1976), *British Birds of Prey*

BROWN, P. (1964), *Birds of Prey*

BROWN, P. and WATERSTON, G. (1962), *The Return of the Osprey*

DENNIS, R. H. and WATERSTON, G. (1973), *Ospreys and Speyside Wildlife*

EVERETT, M. (1975), *Birds of Prey*

GROSSMAN, M. L. and HAMLET, J. (1965), *Birds of Prey of the World*

HARVIE-BROWN, J. A. and MACPHERSON, A. H. (1904), *Fauna of the N.W. Highlands*

INTERNATIONAL COUNCIL FOR BIRD PRESERVATION (1964), Proceedings of Working Conference on Birds of Prey and Owls held at Caen, April 1964

MACKENZIE, O. (1921), *A Hundred Years in the Highlands*

ST JOHN, C. (1849), *Tour in Sutherlandshire*

WATERSTON, G. (1961), *Notes on the breeding biology of the Speyside Ospreys—1959 and 1960*. Bird Notes. Vol. 29

WITHERBY, H. F., JOURDAIN, F. C. R., TICEHURST, N. F. and TUCKER, B. W. (1939), *The Handbook of British Birds*. Vol. III

Index